LIVING WITH
ARTS &
CRAFTS

LIVING WITH
ARTS &
CRAFTS

ROS BYAM SHAW

consultant SU BACON

with photography by ANDREW WOOD

RYLAND
PETERS
& SMALL

London New York

First published in the USA in 2001
by Ryland Peters & Small, Inc.
519 Broadway
5th Floor
New York, NY 10012
www.rylandpeters.com
10 9 8 7 6 5 4 3 2 1

Library of Congress
Cataloging-in-Publication Data

Byam Shaw, Ros.
  Living with Arts & crafts / Ros Byam Shaw
     p. cm.
  Includes index
  ISBN 1-84172-203-0
  1. Interior decoration--United States--History--
  20th century. 2. Arts and crafts movement--
  Influence. I. Title: Living with Arts and crafts.
  II. Title.
  NK2004.B96 2001
  747.213'09'04--dc21
                                    2001031881

Jacket picture credits
Front An Apartment in New York designed by
Stephen Shadley. **Back** Anthony & Julia Collett's
house in London designed by Anthony Collett of
Collett Zarzycki Ltd.

Printed and bound in China.

Senior designer Paul Tilby
Senior editor Henrietta Heald
Location research manager Kate Brunt
Production Patricia Harrington
Art director Gabriella Le Grazie
Publishing director Alison Starling

Stylists Serena Hanbury, Kristin Perers
Proofreader and indexer Laura Hicks

contents

INTRODUCTION

Of all "period" styles, Arts and Crafts must be the easiest to live with—easy because Arts and Crafts furniture is well made and sturdy, not the kind of antique furniture that demands kid-glove treatment and a fence to protect it from dogs and children; easy because the plain, homey designs favored by Arts and Crafts practitioners mix so well with contemporary furniture; and easy because the movement's aesthetic, with its emphasis on simplicity, cozy informality, and "honest" materials, is so in tune with modern taste.

Underlying the practical and versatile beauty of Arts and Crafts design was a preoccupation with form and materials. The essence of the style lies in a love of the handmade and a respect for the natural materials that inspire the craftsman. In the 19th century these twin enthusiasms were compounded by a strong moral dimension, fueled by a distaste for the social effects of industrialization and its mass-produced goods.

"Apart from my desire to produce beautiful things, the leading passion of my life is hatred of modern civilisation," said William Morris. The author and critic John Ruskin described machine-made ornament imitating hand work as "an imposition, an impertinence, and a sin." The architect and designer William Lethaby agreed: "It is the pretence and subterfuge of most machine-made things which make them disgusting." Today we would be hard pressed to muster the same outrage, but we, too, need a respite from the manufactured and the artificial.

To an extent that our Victorian ancestors would have found unimaginable, we are surrounded by machines that shape and dominate our lives. Whether arranging a vacation, e-mailing a friend, or microwaving a dinner, we would not be without machines and the conveniences they bring, but especially in our own homes, we feel ever more keenly the need for human qualities in furnishings and materials. Living with Arts and Crafts means living with objects that have been made by hand, and with natural materials such as wood, leather, and stone—things that reach beyond the purely practical to offer an emotional and aesthetic antidote to too much plastic and too many microchips.

ABOVE Built in the Craftsman style, this house in California's Sierra Nevada Mountains combines Arts and Crafts standards of construction and finish with an open-plan layout and a use of technology that is entirely modern.

RIGHT With its generous leather sofa and Stickley-style spindle chairs, the upstairs living area has the relaxed feel of a gentlemen's club. The walls are lined with plain wooden paneling, stained with two coats of urethane oil. Lamps with art-glass shades and an old-fashioned telephone complete the picture of traditional comfort.

THE
ARTS & CRAFTS
MOVEMENT

WILLIAM MORRIS AND HIS FOLLOWERS WANTED TO DISSOLVE
THE DISTINCTIONS BETWEEN THE FINE AND THE DECORATIVE
ARTS AND BETWEEN THE DESIGNER AND THE CRAFTSMAN.

creating a new
aesthetic

When William Morris commissioned his friend Philip Webb to design a house in the country for him and his new bride, he wanted it to remind him of the Gothic cathedrals he had visited in France. His Red House still stands, its spiky silhouette of steep gables hidden by a green ruff of gardens, orchard, and high hedges. There is now no trace of the small village of Upton. Instead, Red House is surrounded by the suburban sprawl of outer London like a jewel in a box of plastic beads.

Red House is often described as the first Arts and Crafts house, the birthplace of a movement that had a huge influence on the style of domestic architecture and interiors in Britain, America, and, to a lesser degree, continental Europe. Stripped of almost all its original furnishings, the interior of Red House can only hint at the richness that led the poet and painter Dante Gabriel Rossetti to describe it as "more a poem than a house."

Morris's circle included several talented young artists. Making the three-hour journey from London by train and coach, Rossetti, Edward Burne Jones, Ford Madox Brown, and other artistic friends set about decorating the "Towers of Topsy," as they called it, painting the pitched roofs of the upstairs rooms with simple repeating patterns, designing stained glass for the windows and tiles to line the porch, and embellishing the giant pieces of built-in furniture with Pre-Raphaelite paintings of knights and damsels.

It was this experience of collaborative interior decoration that inspired Morris in 1861 to launch the firm first known as Morris, Marshall, Faulkner and Co., and later simply as Morris and Co. The aim was to supply furnishings of all kinds, from tables to murals, from metalwork to stained glass, designed by artists and handmade by craftsmen.

Inspired by the writings of Augustus Pugin and John Ruskin—both of whom revered the Middle Ages as a time when art and craft went hand in glove—Morris sought to dissolve the distinctions between the fine and the decorative arts and between the designer and the craftsman.

One of the most successful of the company's lines, the "Sussex" chair, was designed by the artist Rossetti. Morris himself, having briefly trained as an

ABOVE This small Voysey house is furnished with spare and elegant period pieces, as the architect would have wished.

OPPOSITE In the kitchen of the same house, time seems to have stood still. The original Triplex range, still used as a fireplace, retains its original surround with extra-high overmantel, again designed by Voysey.

AT THE HEART OF THE MOVEMENT'S PHILOSOPHY WAS A ROSE-TINTED NOSTALGIA FOR THE LATE MIDDLE AGES.

ABOVE The Arroyo Huntington hanging light echoes the simple geometry of stair rails and window on the landing of an original Craftsman house of 1917.

architect and tried his hand as a painter, discovered a rare genius for pattern which he applied to wallpapers, fabrics, tapestries, embroideries, and carpets.

A rose-tinted nostalgia for the late Middle Ages was key to the philosophy of the movement. "Our Gothic Revival," wrote Morris's pupil John Sedding in 1893, "has enriched the crafts by impetus and imitation . . . It has been the health-giving spark—the ozone of modern art." Gothic art and architecture were seen as representing a national, homegrown style, morally superior to foreign imports. The working methods of medieval carpenters were praised as "honest." The marks of adze on wood, chisel on stone, and hammer on metal were admired as evidence of "the sense of human labour and care." Compared with the earlier Gothic Revival, the Arts and Crafts movement was more concerned to capture in its buildings and interiors the spirit rather than the letter of Gothic style, the aim being to come up with an equivalent but entirely modern vernacular.

A reverence for the products of a pre-industrial past was matched by a belief that architecture, the home, and its furnishings had a profound moral influence on both the individual and society. When Americans embraced the ideas of Morris and Ruskin, they adopted and adapted the Arts and Crafts search for a national style by rediscovering their own vernacular in the log cabins of the pioneers, the shingles and verandas of colonial architecture, and the white-painted adobe buildings of the Spanish missions. Gustav Stickley promoted his "Craftsman" furniture as expressing "the fundamental sturdiness and directness of the American point of view."

In Britain and North America, Morris was a figurehead for the artists and intellectuals, architects, and designers who wanted to clean up Victorian design. His message was clear: "Have nothing in your house that you do not know to be useful or believe to be beautiful." It was often repeated; for example, the *Art Journal* of 1892 told the reader "not to increase the number of household goods, but to make a clean sweep of the lot and to supply their place with the few objects, plain, well designed and well made, that we require for actual use."

Following the example of Morris, likeminded designers and makers formed groups to market and sell their work. The title of "guild," with its medieval resonance, was thought appropriate for such a group.

In 1882 the Century Guild was set up; hot on its heels came the Art Workers' Guild of 1884 and the Guild of Handicrafts of 1887. In 1888, 27 years after Morris first sent out the prospectus for his firm, the Arts and Crafts Exhibition Society was created, providing an outlet for the work of many leading practitioners of the movement, and a name for their style that has stuck ever since.

Contemporary photographs of popular late-Victorian interiors graphically reveal what the reformers were up against. Even in muted black and white, the effect of these rooms—crammed with furniture, bristling with pattern, festooned with fringe and drapery—is smothering. The same room might encompass a bewildering array of style pastiches: a neoclassical fireplace, a mock-Tudor ceiling, a Mooresque fretwork arch, a pseudo-Baroque sideboard, and so on. For the grandest interiors, expensive copies of 18th-century French furnishings were the height of fashion, disparagingly referred to as *Le style tous-les-Louis.*

Charles Eastlake, whose 1868 book *Hints on Household Taste in Furniture, Upholstery and Decoration* ran to seven editions in the U.S., promoted a simple, medieval-inspired style described by one admiring critic as "inaugurating a new regime which bears the same relation to the loose and wanton Quartorze and Quinze regimes that virtue bears to vice." Morality aside, the contrast between traditional Victorian interiors and those designed by the avant-garde who took their lead from Morris is striking.

Two English architects of the late Victorian era whose work was of seminal importance were Sir Edwin Lutyens

ABOVE A Napoleon chair, after a design by Lutyens, stands in the corner of a landing overlooking the great hall at Little Thakeham. The house is also by Lutyens.

and C.F.A. Voysey, both of whom were strongly influenced by Arts and Crafts ideas. Voysey, whose talent for design embraced wallpapers and fabrics as well as furniture and fixtures, was particularly concerned with aesthetic unity, and keen to exert control over the interior of a house as well as over its structure.

A client who commissioned a house from Voysey would move into a building already supplied with specially designed handles, latches, hinges, and even towel rods, shelving, and built-in furniture. For those rare commissions that included

THE MARKS OF ADZE ON WOOD, CHISEL ON STONE, AND HAMMER ON METAL WERE ADMIRED AS EVIDENCE OF "THE SENSE OF HUMAN LABOUR AND CARE."

furnishings, Voysey would plot positions for his pieces on the floor plan. Old photographs and watercolor sketches of pure Voysey rooms show interiors of supreme elegance and restraint.

Although he designed furniture for some of his houses, Lutyens was less concerned about total control. Later in his career, his architectural style veered toward a rather grandiose Palladianism and neo-Georgianism, but his early houses—such as Munstead Wood, built for the garden designer Gertrude Jekyll, and Little Thakeham in Sussex— have a solid, simple, old-English vernacular feel inside and out. Wide oak floorboards, planked oak doors with forged metal latches, and hefty internal beams are complemented by plain white or stone walls and stone-mullioned windows.

On the other side of the Atlantic, the brothers Charles and Henry Greene were developing an idiosyncratic style, a blend of Japanese and Scandinavian architectural motifs, which was to be as influential in North America as Voysey and Lutyens were in England. In common with Voysey, the Greenes liked to design their houses inside and out, creating rooms rich with beautifully crafted wood and glowing with art-glass panels and lighting, and specifying Craftsman furniture by Gustav Stickley or designing their own. The Gamble House, commissioned from the Greenes in 1907 and preserved complete with its custom-made furnishings, remains the most famous and most widely imitated example of Arts and Crafts architecture in the U.S. Stickley's *The Craftsman*

ABOVE LEFT Today's range is the modern equivalent of an Arts and Crafts stove with none of the fuss.

ABOVE RIGHT Every room in this Voysey cottage, bedrooms included, has an original fire surround with period tiles. The light oak chair is a Charliero copy of a Voysey original.

OPPOSITE Plain ceramic tiles laid flat on a chimney breast with a simple overmantel were a staple of Arts and Crafts design on both sides of the Atlantic. This modern interpretation adds an asymmetrical twist.

WRIGHT UNDERSTOOD THE EMOTIONAL VALUE OF THE HANDMADE, AND OF NATURAL MATERIALS SENSITIVELY AND LOVINGLY EMPLOYED.

ABOVE LEFT For a masculine, quirky look that is very up to date, the designer Stephen Shadley has mixed original pieces with the work of modern craftsmen and designers.

ABOVE CENTER The pinstriped verticals of Arts and Crafts spindle chairs are typical of furniture by Stickley and Lloyd Wright, both of whom liked to see oak cut straight.

ABOVE RIGHT The square metal lantern hung from a chain was a popular light fixture in the U.S. and is still widely reproduced.

magazine, to which the Greene brothers were early subscribers, became the mouthpiece of the Arts and Crafts movement in the U.S., while his line of Craftsman furniture embodied the Arts and Crafts desire "to do away with all needless ornamentation, returning to plain principles of construction."

By a judicious use of assembly-line production combined with strict quality control, Stickley was able to make his designs affordable for the ordinary middle-class householder. Stickley's style became so popular that it was much imitated, often at the expense of quality. His Craftsman line was plagiarized even by his brothers, Leopold and George, also furniture makers—but with none of the pride in construction that was so central to Gustav's philosophy.

In England the more accessible end of Arts and Crafts was best represented by the furniture designs of Ambrose Heal. Like Stickley, Heal was not averse to using machinery when appropriate, but he would not compromise by using veneers to mask cheap

wood or by using plywood where it didn't show. Furniture by Ambrose Heal and Gustav Stickley was produced in relatively large quantities and can still be found today at reasonable prices. The work of both men has stood the test of time remarkably well, as have their solid methods of construction.

The best modern interpretations of Arts and Crafts style find this same middle ground where the virtues of the machine-made can be accommodated without sacrificing the pleasures of craftsmanship and the beauty of natural materials. This is the ground occupied by Frank Lloyd Wright, whose bold, original brand of "organic" architecture swept Arts and Crafts deep into the 20th century. Wright embraced the mass-produced as a means by which "the poor as well as the rich may enjoy beautiful surface treatments of clean, strong forms," but he also understood the emotional value of the handmade, and of natural materials sensitively and lovingly employed: intangibles that remain at the heart of our appreciation of Arts and Crafts.

THIS PAGE The style is brought right up to date in this huge open-plan living space, where original Arts and Crafts pieces are incorporated into uncompromisingly modernist surroundings. Furnishings are a bold mix of old and new, and the geometric pendant light fixture is a copy of a famous Frank Lloyd Wright design.

THE ROOMS

ARTS AND CRAFTS ARCHITECTS CAME CLOSER THAN THEIR LESS ADVENTUROUS CONTEMPORARIES TO CREATING INTERIORS THAT WE WOULD FEEL HAPPY WITH TODAY.

VERSATILE AND COMFORTABLE
living rooms

LEFT This Greene and Greene house is furnished in a style that is far from strict Arts and Crafts, but retains its spirit. The chandelier is inspired by one at Greene and Greene's Duncan-Irwin House.

ABOVE RIGHT In the living room with its unusual stepped brick fireplace, Arts and Crafts lighting and a high-backed settle share the space with more urbane pieces.

We do more living in our living rooms than our 19th-century ancestors did. In Victorian times, people were specific about how rooms were used. A house with several "receiving" rooms would have a dining room for eating and a morning room with a desk for use in the morning; there might also be a library and a billiard room. Arts and Crafts architects tended to follow this traditional division, and included in their houses the formal drawing room —a room to be used in the afternoon, for "at homes," and tea parties, and in the evening for withdrawing after dinner.

The Victorian drawing room was a feminine place, a setting for the hostess and a showcase for her style, a polite room where precious and elaborate furniture was displayed, including the obligatory grand piano. Humbler households had a parlor with an upright piano, a front room reserved for Sunday best. Such a

strict segregation of rooms is alien to our modern lifestyle. Today's living room is a shared, multifunctional space. While it remains a place for entertaining, it is also a room used by all the family, whether for watching television, reading a newspaper, using a computer, or listening to music. Modern designs for living spaces often incorporate cooking and dining areas in the living room. Arts and Crafts architects came closer than their less adventurous contemporaries to creating the kind of interiors we would feel comfortable in today. Designers such as Edwin Lutyens, Philip Webb, and M. H. Baillie Scott were

RADICAL SIMPLIFICATION MADE THE ARTS AND CRAFTS LIVING ROOM A FAR MORE PRACTICAL SPACE THAN THE OVERFULL, BRIC-A-BRAC DEPOSITORIES OF CONVENTIONAL TASTE.

innovators with a democratic bent who challenged some of the strict hierarchies of Victorian society and design. Although they included separate drawing rooms in their plans, they also added another, more casual reception room, the "living hall." Based on the idea of the medieval great hall, this was a room more akin to our modern idea of a living room: a central, communal space, of no fixed purpose,

warmed by a huge fireplace and furnished with
comfortable chairs. The living hall at Standen
in West Sussex proved so popular for tea parties
and musical evenings that the house's architect,
Philip Webb, extended it by adding a bay window
and an alcove to accommodate the family piano.

Illustrations by Baillie Scott for magazines such
as *The Studio* did much to popularize this new type
of room, showing a variety of schemes for idealized
living halls. Few of Baillie Scott's schemes were put

into effect, but the idea of the living hall was widely
adopted for suburban houses in the Arts and Crafts
tradition. These were living halls on a modest scale,
very often fitted out with built-in furniture, deep
window seats padded with flat cushions, and settles
built around the fireplace to create that fashionable
feature, the "cozy corner."

The "living hall" exemplified the Arts and Crafts
rebellion against rigid convention. Even in the
formal drawing room, the impetus was to create

OPPOSITE Built in 1910 by Charles Edward Bateman, this house has original features such as ceiling beams and paneling. True to Arts and Crafts tradition, new furnishings and fixtures such as the glass-and-metal lights were commissioned from craftsmen/designers.

THIS PICTURE An inner hall is lined with panels of original stained glass by Morris & Co. and reproduction stained glass based on designs by Edward Burne-Jones.

a relaxed environment. Radical simplification, the clearing of clutter, and the stripping away of heavy draperies made the Arts and Crafts living room a far more practical and usable space than the overstuffed, overfull, bric-a-brac depositories of conventional taste.

In North America, the term "living room" was already in use before the Arts and Crafts movement took root. In Gustav Stickley's vision of the ideal family home, promoted in his magazine *The Craftsman*, the living room was "a place where work is to be done . . . the haven of rest . . . the place where children grow and thrive." This description is in tune with 21st-century ideas, but Stickley goes on to insist: "It is here that we should be our best," suggesting that he might not approve of supper in front of the television, or any number of lax modern habits.

A neat visual summary of the difference between mainstream taste and the type of reformed interior promoted by Arts and Crafts designers is provided by a pair of illustrations from the December 1904 issue of *The Craftsman*. Accompanying an article baldly entitled "From Ugliness to Beauty," these are "before" and "after" views of a modest, middle-class parlor. "Before" features lacy curtains, a loud wallpaper topped by an even louder frieze, a patterned ceiling, buttoned upholstery, and heavily carved, curvy furniture in neo-Renaissance style. This crowded, feminine decor is replaced in the "after" picture with plain, unlined curtains, plain walls with a deep frieze of stylized trees, a leather armchair, and a wooden settle. Gilt-framed pictures and overmantel have been replaced by a single, rather austere print and a plain mantel clock. There

LEFT The owners of a grand old shingle house on New York's Fisher Island, built in Queen Anne style in the early 1930s, have furnished and decorated its interior with their collection of antique and reproduction American Arts and Crafts. The wooden ceiling beams are original and give the downstairs living room the feel of a much earlier house. Pale upholstery and embroidered and appliquéd pillows are matched by a rug in a Frank Lloyd Wright design with a cream background. Open shelving displays a collection of pottery, both old and new.

THE PIECES ARE CHARACTERIZED BY SUCH A SIMPLE, RATIONAL STYLE OF DESIGN THAT THEY WOULD LOOK EQUALLY AT HOME IN A KITCHEN, A LIVING ROOM, A HALL, OR EVEN A PLAYROOM.

LEFT AND RIGHT Apart from the upholstered tub armchairs, the furniture in the living room of this Pasadena bungalow, built in 1913, is in the robust, masculine style of Gustav Stickley and his disciples.

Antique and reproduction rub shoulders here. The oak settle is an original Craftsman piece, newly upholstered in black leather, while the Tiffany-style table lamp with its art-glass shade is new.

is an interesting parallel here between the cluttered, chintzy interiors that were so chic nearly one hundred years later, in the 1980s, and the pared-down, more masculine look that has superseded them. Modern eyes find more to admire in Stickley's makeover than in the pretty jumble of "before"—which appears as old-fashioned to us as it did to Stickley.

These same illustrations reveal another Arts and Crafts innovation that we now appreciate. Not only is the redecorated parlor less crowded, but also the three pieces of furniture it contains—a wood-framed settle, a leather armchair, and a circular side table—are of such simple, rational design that they would look equally at home in a kitchen, a living room, a hall, or even a playroom. Today we admire integrated interiors—flooring that flows from room to room and a coherence of style that links our kitchens, dining, and living rooms, even when they are separated by walls and doors.

The elaborate Victorian furniture that characterized the conventional parlor was separated by a stylistic gulf from the more humble furnishings designed for a kitchen

THIS PICTURE The living room of the Duncan-Irwin House, built by Greene and Greene in 1903, has a rare collection of American Arts and Crafts furniture, including pieces by Gustav Stickley, cabinet maker Charles Rohlfs, and others made at the Roycroft community in East Aurora, New York, where there were workshops producing furniture, metalware, stained glass, and books.

A CENTRAL COMMUNAL SPACE OF NO FIXED PURPOSE, THE "LIVING HALL" WAS AKIN TO OUR IDEA OF THE LIVING ROOM.

in the same house. There would be no mistaking the distinction between, for example, the kitchen table with its scrubbed pine top and the mirror-shine mahogany of the dining table. Arts and Crafts furnishings are more democratic and therefore more versatile. An Arts and Crafts dining table in lightly waxed oak, simple and robust, looks at home either in a modern kitchen or in the dining area of a modern living room.

Although the Arts and Crafts living room was informal, it was not necessarily more comfortable than the traditional interior it replaced. Rejecting the fat, buttoned upholstery that bulged and jostled in less avant-garde drawing rooms, William Morris took an uncompromising line. "If you want to be comfortable go to bed," he retorted. Contemporary photographs and drawings

ABOVE Bold shapes and strong silhouettes define this Craftsman living room.

OPPOSITE This 1950s ranch-style home with its plain stone fireplace and chunky mantel-shelf has been remodeled in the style of Greene and Greene. It has the feel of an authentic Craftsman creation.

of the purist Arts and Crafts interior show drawing rooms sparsely furnished with thinly padded wood-framed chairs and settles. The visual effect of clean lines and straight edges is attractive, but you can search in vain for somewhere to slump.

Gustav Stickley was more conciliatory on the subject of comfort than his mentor Morris, declaring: "The best way to get something better [is] to go directly back to plain principles of construction and apply them to the making of simple, strong, comfortable furniture." In fact, upholstered armchairs from Morris & Co. are no less comfortable than Stickley's padded reclining chairs.

Original Arts and Crafts furniture may not satisfy the modern demand for sofas squashy enough to snooze on, but today's upholstery can offer clean, straight lines combined with springs and padding for the best of both worlds. Indeed, there are many ways in which Arts and Crafts style and today's aesthetic can complement one another. Many Arts and Crafts designs still look modern more than a century after they left the drawing board. In particular, Stickley's Craftsman line of furniture has a robust, square-edged simplicity. Apart from patina, his graceful spindle chairs, slatted settles, and tables with keyed tenon joints are barely distinguishable from some of the restrained, unpretentious furniture made by today's designer–craftsmen. Squashy sofas aside, it would be quite

THIS PAGE The double-height, open-plan living area of this traditionally built post-and-beam house is reminiscent of the great halls of the grander Arts and Crafts country house. Hanging metal lanterns and the Stickley-style oak dining table and chairs complement the rugged simplicity of the architecture, with its emphasis on wood and the skills of the carpenter.

possible, if prohibitively expensive, to fill your modern living room with antique Arts and Crafts furniture and feel you lacked nothing: side tables, desks, table and floor lamps, glass-fronted cabinets for the display of china, cushions, rugs.

Arts and Crafts pieces can be mixed equally successfully with furniture from other periods and cultures. Arts and Crafts designers themselves took inspiration from antiques, particularly from the beautifully crafted, country-made furniture of the 18th century and from Japanese design. Shaker furniture sits well with chunkier Arts and Crafts pieces, as does some of the restrained antique

ABOVE Reproductions of Frank Lloyd Wright designs, including the sofa with built-in shelf, the lamp, and the barrel chairs, furnish this 1940s house in Los Angeles. The designs look as fresh as they did on the day when they left the architect's drawing board. The motto of the house's original owners is spelled out in hammered copper lettering under the stone overmantel.

Chinese furniture in vogue in the early 21st century. Cane or willow chairs add a note of levity. Original pieces by the Dryad company are rare and expensive, but there is no lack of modern versions. There is scope, as there always was, for a wide variety of tastes within the Arts and Crafts tradition.

There is one feature without which even the most modern version of an Arts and Crafts living room would feel incomplete. Long before the magnetic flicker of the television screen came to dominate our rooms, the dancing flames in the fireplace had the same mesmeric effect, drawing the gaze while providing the added comfort of

STICKLEY'S GRACEFUL SPINDLE CHAIRS AND
SLATTED SETTLES ARE BARELY DISTINGUISHABLE
FROM SOME OF TODAY'S RESTRAINED PIECES.

warmth. Traditional Victorian fireplaces were decorated with
elaborate gilt overmantels, grand mantel clocks, and fringed
draperies. Arts and Crafts designers were no less eager to
emphasize this focus and symbol of family life. Indeed, they
were particularly sensitive to the importance of the fireplace
in establishing a sense of welcome, and found various ways to
accentuate its effect without resort to mirrors or draperies.

A favorite Arts and Crafts archetype was the inglenook, with
its broad mantel and capacious hearth. Where space and scale
allowed, architects such as M.H. Baillie Scott and E.S. Prior
made their inglenooks big enough to incorporate seating. The
inglenook that spreads across one wall of the drawing room in
the Gamble House embraces a pair of settles, glass-fronted
cabinets, and a table, making it more a room within a room
than a fireplace. Massive hoods were another way to draw
attention to this centerpiece of a room. Stickley used copper;
Bernard Maybeck used stone. Also popular, and less grandiose,
was the tiled surround that used plain glazed tiles, often in
modulating shades of the same color, to cover the chimney breast
up to the level of a high wooden mantelshelf supported
on brackets. This type of fireplace can be adapted to suit any
modern room and is relatively easy to recreate.

LEFT Dark cabinets flanking a
chimney breast bring the Arts
and Crafts tradition of built-in
furniture into a former carriage
house in New York. The slim
spindles of the Stickley-style
chairs are echoed in the
staircase screen designed by
Stephen Shadley.

OPPOSITE The studio in the garden of designer
Anthony Collett's London home was built by
him as a place for his wife, textile designer Julia
Pines, to work, and as a venue for exhibitions
and parties. The chairs, which have a feel of
chinoiserie, are probably by E.W. Godwin; the
table is Scottish Arts and Crafts, and the chaise-
stool is by Collett. A David Bailey photograph
of the Kray brothers is propped against the wall.

BOTH PICTURES Built in the Arts and Crafts style in 1906 by the Revd. Oliphant, an amateur architect, this country house is now the home of the British designer Sheila Scholes. It had been used as a nursing home and was dark and dingy, with black paintwork, but some original features have survived, including the swooping copper hood and graceful built-in settles. White paint and furnishings of oriental restraint have transformed the house into an entirely modern home without any loss of charm.

ARTS AND CRAFTS FURNITURE IS WONDERFULLY ADAPTABLE—AS APPROPRIATE FOR A CASUAL FAMILY BRUNCH AS FOR AN ELEGANT BANQUET.

SIMPLE AND INVITING
dining rooms

LEFT A modern table and chairs grace the dining room of a 1917 Craftsman house in Pasadena. Like the chain-hung chandelier with handblown shades, the furniture is inspired by Arts and Crafts originals.

ABOVE RIGHT Hanging lights above the dining table are a familiar Arts and Crafts feature. Light fixtures with art-glass shades in glowing colors make an eye-catching focus in this modern, Craftsman-style, post-and-beam house in the Sierra Nevada Mountains.

RIGHT Carved decoration on furniture such as this English dining chair is typically flat and minimal.

FAR RIGHT A George V club armchair, upholstered in soft burgundy leather, shares the dining chair's solid construction and promise of comfort.

Throughout the 19th century and well into the 20th, the dining room was considered an essential of civilized living. Many a small row house had a room split into drawing room and dining room so that, even if the family could afford to employ only a daily maid-of-all-work, she could serve the dinner she had prepared in the kitchen while they sat in state at the linen-draped table.

Slowly but surely, the dining room has been falling out of favor ever since. Nowadays, almost all of us cook, sometimes because we enjoy it. If

we don't like cooking, we can buy any number of ready-made meals, order a delivery or indulge in the pleasure of eating out in a restaurant, when we, too, can sit in state and be waited on.

Dining at home is an increasingly informal activity. Heedless of the once-hallowed daily ritual of the communal meal, many families rarely eat together, perhaps convening at the table only at weekends or for special occasions. As a result, the separate dining room tends to have the cold, unloved feel of a room with no real purpose.

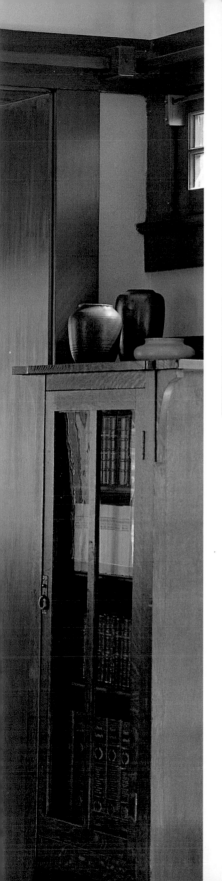

LEFT The dining room of the Duncan-Irwin House in Pasadena is still lit by its original chandelier, a design that has been much copied and adapted by modern lovers of Craftsman style. The influence of Japanese architecture and art is seen in the crisscross pattern of beams decorating the chimney breast.

ABOVE LEFT AND RIGHT A patinated copper screen with glowing landscape panels forms the backdrop for informal dining in a newly built seaside home on the Pacific Central Coast. The dining chairs are new, with fine inlays inspired by the designs of Harvey Ellis, Gustav Stickley's chief designer.

The average Victorian dining room was in continual use and the scene of rigid conventions, from the seating plan to the order and manner in which food was served and presented. The shiny mahogany table was always clad in a shroud of crisp, starched damask, and family portraits stared down from the walls.

Arts and Crafts designers were nonconformists. They enjoyed bending the rules, and in many cases were the first of their generation to introduce practices that later became universal. Take the tablecloth. Recalling some years later a visit to William Morris's house in Hammersmith, west London, in the 1880s, George Bernard Shaw wrote: "On the supper table there was no table cloth: a thing common enough now . . . but then an innovation so staggering that it cost years of domestic conflict to introduce it." Even more unconventionally, Morris would set up a long oak table in his drawing room for special occasions, laying it with green glass and blue china, reviving the 18th-century habit of setting up table wherever it was most convenient.

In North America, the tablecloth was transformed into what came to be known as the table scarf—a strip of plain cream fabric, usually linen, longer than the table for which it was designed, but narrow enough to leave the table top bare on each side. The overhang at each end was often embroidered with a simplified organic motif. Drawings of idealized Craftsman interiors from

LEFT AND FAR LEFT A contemporary table and chairs blend well with the wood-paneled dining room of a 1919 Craftsman house.

BELOW The open-plan dining area of a beach house in the style of Greene and Greene opens onto a deck with ocean views.

RIGHT This Greene and Greene house has furniture with an oriental feel, in keeping with the influences that shaped its architecture.

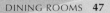

CHAIRS AND TABLES WERE BASED ON COUNTRY
AND COTTAGE STYLES; PARTICULARLY POPULAR WAS THE
REFECTORY TABLE, DATING FROM THE MIDDLE AGES.

Stickley's magazine show tables in dining rooms and living rooms draped with these scarves, the only bare-topped exceptions being small side tables. One illustration offers an ingenious arrangement of three table scarves: a long central one and two shorter narrower scarves running across the table at right angles to it, neatly providing four place settings.

Apart from the table and the set of matching dining chairs, the other fixture of the Arts and Crafts dining room was the sideboard. In grander Victorian households this was where the butler carved the meat, and it was also the resting place for decanters, the soup tureen, and the vegetable dishes, which were never left on the table as they are today. Arts and Crafts sideboards

ABOVE New York designer Stephen Shadley's version of Arts and Crafts style is uncompromisingly modern, picking up on the elements of oriental design that were so much a part of Greene and Greene's repertoire.

RIGHT The same oriental influences can be seen in Anthony Collett's London dining room in the original Heal's chairs, which are set around a table first designed by Heal's for Winston Churchill. The oak settles and dark marble-tiled fireplace were made to Collett's own designs.

were frequently built in, sometimes into an alcove with an art-glass window above, as in the Gamble House. The freestanding sideboard—designed to be just the right height to serve from—with its combination of shelved cupboards and drawers remains an extremely useful piece of furniture.

Arts and Crafts designers went a long way toward making the dining room less formal and stuffy—such a long way that most Arts and Crafts dining furniture suits very well our modern preference for cooking and eating in the same room. In fact, Arts and Crafts designers often took inspiration for their dining furniture from the kitchen—for

example, adapting the hutch for use as a sideboard: an elevation of a humble piece of furniture from servants' quarters to receiving room that was almost as radical as their rejection of the tablecloth. Chairs and tables came in designs based on country and cottage furniture. The refectory table, a form dating back to the Middle Ages, was particularly popular, the construction of its plain, planked top sometimes emphasized by the use of "butterfly" joints.

Another favorite Arts and Crafts design was the rush-seated ladderback chair, copied and adapted from traditional country chairs by Ernest Gimson and Charles Ashbee among others. An Arts and Crafts quirk, taken to outlandish extremes by Charles Rennie

Mackintosh, was to give chairs exaggeratedly high backs. Many of Voysey's designs for furniture are characterized by tall tapering verticals, and he liked to make the backs of his dining chairs particularly lofty for the master and mistress of the house, who were traditionally seated at either end of the table.

Dining chairs by Gustav Stickley and Ambrose Heal tend to be more conventionally proportioned. Both made dining furniture that is still copied, used, and loved today. Handsome as well as unassuming, it is furniture that bridges that awkward gap between kitchen informality and the requirements of elegant dining, as appropriate for a messy family brunch as for an elegant evening banquet.

ABOVE, LEFT AND RIGHT Comfortable, solid, elegant, but not too grand, furniture in the Arts and Crafts style, such as these reproduction Stickley chairs and table, is ideal for informal modern dining.

OPPOSITE Even slightly more extreme pieces—for example, these reproduction Mackintosh dining chairs—can be both practical and stylish.

FREQUENTLY INSPIRED BY KITCHEN FURNITURE, ARTS AND CRAFTS PIECES SUIT VERY WELL OUR MODERN PREFERENCE FOR COOKING AND EATING IN THE SAME ROOM.

COMBINING FORM AND FUNCTION FOR
AN "HONEST" RESULT WITHOUT NEEDLESS
ORNAMENT WAS THE DESIGNERS' MANTRA.

BRIGHT AND CONVENIENT

kitchens

LEFT The capacious porcelain sink and the wooden cupboards and work surfaces in the kitchen of this Greene and Greene house might have been put in yesterday. In fact, all these items are original to the house, making this room a rare survivor.

RIGHT The view of the butler's pantry in the same house shows how Greene and Greene brought innovation and the utmost attention to detail even to the simplest woodwork.

Unlike today's gleaming shrines of stainless steel and oiled cherrywood, the 19th-century kitchen was not built to impress. No particular status attached to its design because nobody who was anybody saw it. In England a morbid distaste for cooking smells banished the kitchen to basements in town, and to far-flung wings in larger country houses. Even in the U.S., where the kitchen was more likely to be next to the dining room, a butler's pantry would be put between them

where space allowed. The kitchen at the Gamble House has the extra precaution of an extractor fan with a giant hood that hangs over the stove ready to spirit away the faintest whiff of bacon.

Modern architects tend to treat the kitchen as the social heart of the home, and site it accordingly. Meanwhile, in period houses, kitchens that would have been in basements are now more likely to occupy rooms once reserved for formal entertaining.

William Morris's brand of Arts and Crafts philosophy included a strong socialist element, which meant that the typical Arts and Crafts kitchen was reasonably well situated and well appointed.

THE ARTS AND CRAFTS KITCHEN HAD
A CENTRAL TABLE WITH A SCRUBBED
PINE TOP FOR FOOD PREPARATION.

For example, Red House, designed for Morris by
Philip Webb, broke with convention by offering
views of the garden from its kitchens—a rare
privilege for cooks and scullery maids. One of
Philip Webb's later houses, Clouds, built for the
Wyndham family, was partially destroyed by fire
just two years after its completion. The family
moved into the undamaged servants' wing, and
Mrs. Wyndham wrote to a friend, "It is a good
thing that our architect was a Socialist, because
we find ourselves just as comfortable in the
servants' quarters as we were in our own."

Idealism aside, it was increasingly important in
the late 19th century to provide a pleasant working
environment for servants. Factories offered an
alternative and more independent means of earning
a living, so finding and keeping skilled and reliable
staff was a constant preoccupation. A good cook
was a particular treasure. Mary Gamble valued her
cook so highly that she entrusted her with the
design of the kitchen in the new house she and her
husband commissioned from Greene and Greene.
The result is bright and airy, lined with white tiles
and including as many mod cons as were available.

The mod cons of a hundred years ago seem far
from convenient in an age when the elbow grease
has been removed from almost every kitchen task
by an array of gadgets and a battery of machines.
Gadgets aside, when Arts and Crafts architects were
given free rein the kitchens they designed were

ABOVE Matt glazed tiling in earthy colors, hanging lanterns, and art-glass lighting give this kitchen a strong Arts and Crafts flavor, accentuated by the use of natural wood. Even the fluorescent ceiling lights are encased in wood and glass.

LEFT The breakfast bar in this spacious kitchen has been reinterpreted in the Craftsman style, complete with rush-seated bar stools. The shiny stainless steel of the sink, eye-level oven, and extractor hood introduce sharp slices of modernity.

OPPOSITE, TOP TO BOTTOM Handmade wooden kitchens in the style of Greene and Greene can be seen in many different guises. Authentic Arts and Crafts details include hand-forged metal handles and dovetail joints.

TOP AND ABOVE Inspired by Arts and Crafts, the architect of this modern lodge in the Idaho mountains has achieved design unity by the consistent use of natural materials and repeated motifs. The raised wooden checkerboard panels used to decorate cupboard and drawer fronts in the kitchen reappear throughout the house at the corners of each wooden window frame.

ABOVE AND LEFT The chunky oak doors in Anthony Collett's kitchen were salvaged from a Victorian vestry and fitted with handles made by a blacksmith to a design by the owner. Complementing them are paneled built-in cabinets and dark marble work surfaces.

handsome and practical. Combining form and function for an "honest" design that would exclude unnecessary ornament was an Arts and Crafts mantra. Stickley summed it up in his repeated statement that "A chair, a table, a bookcase or bed [must] fill its mission of usefulness as well as it possibly can." He applied the same principle to a room, which could be satisfying "only when it completely fulfills the purpose for which it is intended."

The kitchens at Lutyens's Castle Drogo in Devon are a case in point, a glorious marriage of pragmatism and aesthetics, with floors that alternate between oak and flagstones, and chunky oak

THIS PICTURE Plain white tiles, hammered metal drawer pulls, and antique glass handles enhance the period feel of an original 1917 Craftsman bungalow.

BELOW LEFT AND RIGHT Large porcelain sinks and period-style fixtures such as the hanging lamp with glass shade are widely reproduced.

THIS PICTURE Despite the gleaming stove, this bright American kitchen with its glass-fronted cupboards and ranks of drawers recalls a butler's pantry in an Edwardian country house.

LEFT The kitchen of this 1913 bungalow was remodeled in 1999 with simple fielded paneled cabinet doors in solid oak, and work surfaces in wood and ceramic tiles. The matt-glazed tiles in shades of dusky green used on the walls are similar to the Grueby tiles that Gustav Stickley recommended for use in Craftsman interiors.

RIGHT The hammered stainless-steel sink is a witty modern take on the Arts and Crafts preference for the obviously handmade.

NATURAL MATERIALS, THE DETAILING OF THE WOODWORK, AND THE MAKING OF A PLACE FOR EVERYTHING ARE ELEMENTS THAT READILY TRANSFER TO A MODERN CONTEXT.

cabinets lining the smooth granite walls. A row of deep ceramic sinks is set into wooden countertops, and a wooden plate rack stretches along the wall above. There is also a huge built-in hutch with a sloping row of hooks for pitchers of graduating size. Everything is designed for a particular purpose, and the result is a set of rooms that are as workmanlike as they are unpretentiously elegant. Although the equipment in these kitchens now seems primitive, Lutyens's use of natural materials, the detailing of the woodwork, and that careful provision of a place for everything, which is still essential to the efficient running of a kitchen, are elements that readily transfer to a modern context.

The Arts and Crafts kitchen may not have been on show, but in many ways its aesthetic is alluring. Natural wood in particular, used for cabinets and work surfaces, brings to a room qualities that Stickley's *The Craftsman* summed up as "permanence, homelikeness and rich warm color." Since natural materials

can be just as hygienic and functional as manmade alternatives, using wood and stone in a kitchen is a way to combine "homelikeness" with efficiency.

Instead of work surfaces, the Arts and Crafts kitchen had a central table with a scrubbed pine top for food preparation. Eating in the kitchen was for servants. The Arts and Crafts architect Detmar Blow tried to put his socialist maxims into practice in the large country house he built for himself by insisting that servants and family should dine together in the kitchen. The social mix didn't work, and he and his wife retreated to the dining room.

Today we prefer our kitchens to be big enough to eat in, whether for family suppers or entertaining guests. In the American Craftsman bungalow, where space was at a premium, we begin to see a room more akin to our modern "living kitchen," its floor planked or covered with new linoleum, its walls tiled in white with a border of blue or green, a shiny enamelled stove taking pride of place, and, beneath the window, a sink—because, unlike the British, Americans felt no need for a scullery.

The Craftsman referred to the kitchen as "the special realm of the housewife and the living room of the whole family." A century later, we may have objections to the label of "housewife," but we do like to live in our kitchens.

MOST ARTS AND CRAFTS BEDROOM FURNITURE STILL MORE THAN SATISFACTORILY FULFILLS THE PURPOSE FOR WHICH IT WAS INTENDED.

FRESH AND RELAXING
bedrooms

LEFT Pretty casement windows screened with stretched voile let light flood into the guest bedroom of a two-story Craftsman house built in 1919. Period oak furnishings are as comfortable as anything made today. The bean-pot lamp has a mica shade.

RIGHT A vase by Janice McDufy for Roycroft Pottery is set on an oak chest-of-drawers. Prominent tenon joints at the corners of the chest typify the way in which Arts and Crafts designers made a decorative virtue out of their traditional construction methods.

Bedroom requirements have changed little in the past century. We may need more hanging space than the average Victorian, and we may use a washstand without its jug and basin as a bedside table, but armoires, chests-of-drawers, and dressing tables are as useful as they ever were. The only piece of original Arts and Crafts bedroom furniture unlikely to suit modern needs is the double bed. Single beds were far more common—married couples often chose twin beds—and original double beds are much narrower than modern king and queen sizes. C.F.A. Voysey's own single bed has a monklike austerity in width as well as design, and today looks better suited to a child than to a full-grown man.

Until the 19th century, bedrooms had been shared space—used for entertaining during the day, with trundle beds for servants and children that could be pulled out at night. In large houses, bedrooms were often downstairs and reached through an enfilade of rooms, giving them all the intimacy of a grand corridor.

By the time Victoria came to the throne, bedrooms had moved upstairs, and although they remained the places where marriages were consummated, babies born, and illness and death suffered, their decorations were

THIS PICTURE AND OPPOSITE Reproduction Stickley designs in this Greene and Greene house include a bed with an inlay in the style of Harvey Ellis. The beams and cottage-style planked door give the bedroom an almost fairytale quality of country simplicity.

LEFT This strong, elegant bed has been built in the Craftsman style to modern proportions—most period double beds are too narrow to meet our expectations of comfort. The appliquéd pillows are also modern, but feature characteristic Craftsman motifs such as the stylized ginkgoes.

RIGHT All the furnishings in the guest bedroom of this new house in the Sierra Nevada Mountains are new and based on Stickley originals. The dressing table with integral mirror is as useful a piece of bedroom furniture today as it was a hundred years ago.

A CENTURY AFTER THEY WERE DESIGNED, AMBROSE HEAL'S PLAIN PANELED ARMOIRES, STURDY CHESTS-OF-DRAWERS, AND DRESSING TABLES ARE AS DESIRABLE AS THEY EVER WERE.

no longer subject to such public scrutiny. Long regarded as essentially feminine domains, bedrooms in the late 19th century were rooms where light colors predominated. Pretty William Morris wallpapers with pale repeating patterns in soft shades of green and blue were a popular choice for bedrooms, even in houses which bore few other traces of Arts and Crafts style. Woodwork was painted white or cream, giving typical Arts and Crafts bedrooms a particularly contemporary look.

The transition from dark, woody reception rooms to light, airy bedrooms was a feature of the American Craftsman bungalow. The bedroom for Stickley's two daughters at his

"Craftsman Farms" was praised as having "both delicacy and refinement . . . appropriate to the ideal of the modern woman." Charles Rennie Mackintosh took the trend for pale colors in bedrooms to an extreme at Hill House near Glasgow, his masterpiece of interior design, which he built for the publisher Walter Blackie. Even today the rooms he created for the Blackies look outlandish, almost space age—the bedroom in particular, an immaculate conception of white paint, elongated lines, and delicate geometry. Mackintosh's design philosophy was not in accord with the mainstream of Arts and Crafts idealism (Voysey referred to his work as "Spook School"), but his pared-down

ABOVE This 1940s
house in California
combines modern
pieces with Arts and
Crafts glass, pottery,
and lamps.

RIGHT Louvered
doors front a closet
in the same bedroom.

SIMPLE AND SPARSE, THE ARTS AND CRAFTS
BEDROOM WAS WELL SUITED TO THE REGULAR
AIRING AND DISINFECTING THOUGHT NECESSARY.

aesthetic and commitment to total stylistic
unity have often led to his inclusion under
the Arts and Crafts umbrella.

Hermann Muthesius wrote in 1904,
"The bedroom belongs essentially to the
woman and it might almost be said that
the man merely enters it as her guest."
Although a married couple usually shared
a bedroom, when space permitted the
man would have his own territory, an
adjacent dressing room where he was
expected to wash and dress.

Arts and Crafts houses are far more
generous in their provision of dressing
rooms than of bathrooms. In spite of the
ready availability of hot running water,
the washstand with its pitcher and bowl
remained an essential item of bedroom
furniture. The modern equivalent of
the dressing room is the walk-in closet.
Meanwhile, most original dressing
rooms have been neatly converted into
connecting bathrooms.

In terms of style, the Arts and Crafts
bedroom was in tune with Victorian
concerns about hygiene. The discovery
of germs confirmed what doctors had
long suspected—that overcrowded, ill-
ventilated conditions were unhealthy.
Fresh air, especially during sleep, was
thought vital to good health. Charles
and Henry Greene, whose father was a
doctor specializing in respiratory diseases,
provided sleeping porches leading off all
the bedrooms in the houses they designed.

THIS PAGE AND OPPOSITE
Among the most striking
and memorable designs
for early 20th-century
interiors are those at Hill
House near Glasgow
created by Charles
Rennie Mackintosh. Paul
Morgan commissioned a
copy of the Hill House
bedroom for his own
Arts and Crafts house in
Wales, with woodwork
by The Arts and Crafts
Home and stenciled
walls by Gavin Dunn.

Even in the more challenging British climate, sleeping outdoors became a fashionable tonic, and some houses by Voysey and Lutyens also incorporated covered balconies for alfresco beds.

Simple and sparse, the Arts and Crafts bedroom was well suited to the regular airing and disinfecting thought necessary by the careful Victorian housewife.

In an age before efficient vacuum cleaners, wall-to-wall carpets had to be brushed by hand. Bare floorboards with rugs small enough to be taken outside and beaten were much easier to deal with. Similarly, short cotton or linen curtains, as favored by Arts and Crafts designers, were ideal because they could be washed.

Furniture in unpolished oak with few moldings and little fancy ornament could be fumigated when necessary by wiping

them with a rag soaked in kerosene. Even more streamlined was the built-in bedroom furniture made fashionable by Arts and Crafts designers. Bedrooms such as those fitted out by Voysey—which featured floor-to-ceiling cabinets and built-in chests-of-drawers—minimized the places where fluff and dust might collect.

Built-in closets have since become standard fare in bedrooms. However, more often than not, modern built-in closets can be flimsy and ill-designed. By contrast, Arts and Crafts designers approached built-in furnishings with the same attention to detail and insistence on quality that they applied to freestanding pieces of furniture.

Beds were a particular source of worry for the hygiene-conscious Victorians. Metal bedsteads were popular, not only

WOODWORK WAS PAINTED WHITE OR CREAM, GIVING THE TYPICAL BEDROOM A PARTICULARLY CONTEMPORARY LOOK.

because they were cheap and hygienically nonabsorbent but also because they offered fewer nooks and crannies that might harbor bedbugs. Arts and Crafts designers preferred wooden bedsteads on aesthetic grounds.

In 1897 Heal's introduced a plain wooden bedstead with a metal lath frame, and the grip of the metal bedstead began to loosen. Simple bedroom furniture in

chestnut and oak designed by Ambrose Heal was a great commercial success. One hundred years later, his plain paneled armoires, sturdy chests-of-drawers, and dressing tables are as desirable as they ever were. Like Stickley's Craftsman furniture of the same period, they epitomize all that was best about the more accessible end of Arts and Crafts style, as modestly good-looking as they are practical.

Arts and Crafts style did not penetrate into the bathroom in quite the same way as into the other rooms of the house.

The forces influencing bathroom design—driven principally by concerns about health and hygiene—were more powerful than fashion. At the beginning of the Arts and Crafts period, purpose-built bathrooms were a rarity in Britain, but by the end of the 19th century the modern bathroom had been born, complete with its crisp white tiles and chrome-plated fixtures.

By the time *The Decoration of Houses* by Edith Wharton and Ogden Codman was published in 1897, the U.S. was far ahead of Britain in the provision of bathrooms. Some members of the British aristocracy—spoiled by the convenience and comfort of a portable bathtub placed before a roaring bedroom fire and filled and emptied by servants—continued to dismiss bathrooms

OPPOSITE AND ABOVE Bedroom-door hooks in this Greene and Greene house are original, as are basin, bathtub, and toilet in the guest bathroom.

ABOVE RIGHT New woodwork imitates the style of Greene and Greene.

as fit only for the lower classes. Even in modern houses where bathrooms were available, the hip bath, washstand, and chamber pot remained standard bedroom accoutrements.

Americans had no such qualms about the conveniences of modern plumbing, and embraced them with enthusiasm. Even the humblest Craftsman bungalow, with its two bedrooms and no entrance hall, always included a small bathroom.

Houses of equivalent size in Britain continued to rely on tin bathtubs and an outhouse. The Sanitary Reform Movement of the 1850s was slow to have an impact, and most London households did not have a constant water supply until the 1890s. Meanwhile Wharton and Codman were recommending that bathroom walls and floors should be waterproof and commenting that "a tiled floor and a high wainscotting of tiles are now usually seen" in what they called "ordinary houses."

For architects working in the Arts and Crafts tradition, modernity and convenience were important objectives, but the ratio of bathrooms to bedrooms in British Arts and Crafts houses now seems extremely stingy, reflecting as it does the conservative British attitude to ablutions combined with a failure of plumbing technology. Norney in Surrey, which

IMPECCABLY HYGIENIC
bathrooms

Pure white sanitaryware was desirable because it made the faintest smudge of dirt obvious to the vigilant eye.

Voysey designed with seven upstairs bedrooms, two of which have sizeable dressing rooms, has only one bathroom, while Philip Webb's Standen in West Sussex has one bathroom serving twelve second-floor bedrooms. Only Lutyens was more lavish, sometimes including two bathrooms to serve the principal bedrooms, as at Little Thakeham.

IN WHAT WAS POTENTIALLY A CLINICAL ROOM, THE LOVE OF WOOD MIGHT FIND EXPRESSION IN BUILT-IN CABINETS FOR STORAGE AND AIRING LINEN. BATHTUBS WERE SOMETIMES ENCLOSED BY WOODEN PANELING.

The late Victorians developed something of an obsession about hygiene—fuelled by a new awareness about the causes of disease and the processes by which infections were transmitted. Pure white sanitaryware was considered desirable, even essential, because it would render the faintest smudge of dirt obvious to the vigilant eye. Hermann Muthesius, a great enthusiast for the modern bathroom, suggests in his exhaustive survey *The English House* (1904–5) that white bathroom walls have the added advantage that "by contrast our bodies may appear ruddy with health."

White tiles, as promoted by Wharton and Codman for walls, might also be used to cover the floor. Often the only concession to color in this pristine domain of shiny porcelain, chrome, and nickel-plating was a narrow frieze of plain blue or green tiles.

The Arts and Crafts love of wood might find expression in this potentially clinical room in built-in cabinets for storage and airing linen. Bathtubs were sometimes enclosed by wooden paneling. Voysey's floor plans always show them set in corners against the wall. Gradually, however, the idea gained currency that woodwork in a bathroom was not conducive to perfect hygiene, and by the early years of the 20th century, manufacturers

ABOVE, FAR LEFT Finely crafted oak cupboards and drawers give an Arts and Crafts feel to the bathroom in a modern house on the Pacific Central coast. The washbasin mirror is also framed in oak, and the wall lights reproduce an Art Deco design.

ABOVE LEFT The bathroom in this original Craftsman house has white sanitaryware and tiles, and a modern stained-glass panel in the door.

TOP RIGHT Old-fashioned designs can be adapted to take faucets with push-up plugs.

RIGHT Freestanding rolltop baths, now in vogue again, were thought more hygienic than built-in bathtubs because they could be cleaned behind and underneath. White tiles for walls and floor, as in this modern bathroom, were also thought hygienically desirable

LEFT Furnished with rugs, paintings and colonial Arts and Crafts caned chairs, this bathroom and dressing room is a place where it would be tempting to linger far longer than strictly necessary for washing and dressing.

RIGHT An Arts and Crafts washstand finds a natural home in the bathroom of a 16th-century farmhouse.

BELOW RIGHT The white-painted walls and floors are Arts and Crafts hallmarks.

of sanitaryware were starting to make all their bathtubs freestanding so they could be cleaned both inside and out, and underneath.

In the British home, toilets were tucked away in a separate room, the smallest in the house. This habit met with the approval of Muthesius, who commented rather primly that the presence of the toilet "evokes unpleasant associations of ideas." Americans were typically less squeamish, often including a toilet in the bathroom in addition to installing separate toilets and washbasins elsewhere in the home.

In the hundred years since Hermann Muthesius championed the modern bathroom of his day, bathroom fixtures have adopted a myriad of hues, from primrose yellow to avocado, and bathtubs have been molded from plastics and fiberglass and in all shapes from round to triangular. There have been jacuzzi baths and power showers, sunken baths and bidets. But the basics of the bathroom have remained surprisingly constant. Today the white bathroom is again de rigueur, and Victorian designs for bathtubs and washbasins with generous proportions are widely copied.

SOME MEMBERS OF THE BRITISH ARISTOCRACY CONTINUED
TO DISMISS BATHROOMS AS FIT ONLY FOR THE LOWER CLASSES.

LOCAL STONE AND VERNACULAR STYLES WERE
USED BY ARTS AND CRAFTS ARCHITECTS TO
GIVE THEIR BUILDINGS A SENSE OF BELONGING.

EXHILARATING

outdoor
spaces

The relationship between a house and its setting
was a matter of great importance to the Arts and
Crafts architect. A house should be bonded to its
landscape rather than imposed upon it—an idea
taken to its logical extreme by Frank Lloyd Wright
when he cantilevered Falling Water over a waterfall
and allowed boulders forming the rocky outcrop
on which it was built to push through its floor and
form the hearthstones of its central fireplace.

Less radical architects working in the Arts and
Crafts tradition used local stone and vernacular
styles to give their buildings a sense of belonging.
The structure and materials of a house might be
extended into the garden, with low walls and
terraces incorporating planters and urns. Deep
eaves, verandas, and porches provided shady
outdoor rooms. Elsewhere, paved walkways led
through arbors to rustic summerhouses.

As the middle ground between the manmade
and nature, the Arts and Crafts garden played a
crucial role. The extreme formality of the High

ABOVE RIGHT Lighting is
crucial for indoor-outdoor
spaces that are used after
dark, such as the verandas
of this new house in the
Sierra Nevada Mountains.
The Arts and Crafts metal
lanterns are "Evergreen"
from Arroyo Craftsman.

RIGHT This Craftsman-style
post-and-beam house was
built to exploit its setting.
Framed by aspens, it stands
in 5 acres (2 hectares), and
a creek runs through the
land. The porch walls are
built from river rock.

OPPOSITE The outdoor
terrace of a 1913 bungalow
in Pasadena can easily
become an extra room for
dining and entertaining,
furnished with comfortable
wooden chairs and table,
and lit by lanterns hanging
from nearby trees.

Victorian garden with its hard-edged geometry and complicated patterns of planting was rejected in favor of a more natural, cottage-garden look. Vegetable gardens and orchards were integrated rather than hidden away, and parts of larger gardens might be given over to wildflowers.

Some of the most famous and influential gardens of the period were the result of creative collaboration between the architect Sir Edwin Lutyens and the garden designer Gertrude Jekyll. In gardens such as Hestercombe in Somerset, Lutyens designed the layout of arbors and canals, steps and terraces, while Jekyll applied her artist's eye to filling the borders and beds with drifts of color and covering the walls and pillars with rambling roses, vines, and wisteria.

This marriage of hard landscaping—which might be quite formal in its sense of balance, order, and symmetry—and the loose planting favored by garden designers such as Jekyll was typical of the grander Arts and Crafts garden. On a more humble scale, a Craftsman single-story house might squeeze in a meandering path edged with pebbles, a wooden arbor, and even a pond.

As Gustav Stickley's booklet *Craftsman Houses* (1913) explained, we need a garden because "in practically all of us is a deep, distinctive longing to possess a little corner of that green Eden from which our modern and materialistic ways of living have made us exiles."

THE MARRIAGE OF HARD LANDSCAPING AND THE LOOSE PLANTING FAVORED BY GARDEN DESIGNERS SUCH AS GERTRUDE JEKYLL TYPIFIED THE GRANDER STYLE.

LEFT Leading off the main living room of this Craftsman-style house is a roofed open deck, furnished with a Morris rocker upholstered in leather.

RIGHT Capacious wooden chairs and the shade of a deep beamed roof make the terrace a particularly inviting place to sit and enjoy the view.

THE
ELEMENTS

AREAS OF FLAT PAINT IN SHADES OF WHITE
AND CREAM WERE CONTRASTED WITH THE DEEP,
WARM COLORS OF PATTERNED TEXTILES.

THE NATURAL WORLD CAPTURED IN
color, pattern, & motif

OPPOSITE, TOP ROW Gustav Stickley and Frank Lloyd Wright both argued that wood was better straight cut than turned or heavily carved, and one of the most striking characteristics of Craftsman furniture is the repetition of the straight line, especially as vertical ranks of straight spindles. This same pattern of verticals can be seen here repeated as panels within a door, as glazing bars and as banisters.

OPPOSITE, BOTTOM ROW Two modern staircases in the style of Greene and Greene feature the subtle patterns of construction and woodwork that became such as trademark of the brothers' careful style.

The word most often used to promote the Arts and Crafts aesthetic was "honest." Its opposites were defined as artifice, pretension, and over-elaboration. In furniture design these reprehensible qualities might be found in the use of exotic veneers to mask cheap woods or applied decorations in composition and papier-mâché to simulate elaborate carving. In their 1876 book on interior design, the furniture makers Agnes and Rhoda Garrett advised: "Never go out of your way to make a thing or a material look like what it is not." To do so, according to Arts and Crafts principles, was a cheat and a lie.

A reverence for nature was integral to the Arts and Crafts philosophy. Nature was the antidote to the satanic mills of dirty, noisy industry. Natural materials were God-given, and their intrinsic qualities should be respected. Voysey was especially purist: "Carving richly veined marbles and finely figured woods is only the action of irreverence and conceit." When he used marble for a fire surround, he used it in flat slabs to maximize the decorative effect of its grain, and he always stipulated that his furniture should be lightly oiled but never polished.

LEFT The mantelshelf in a room by Mark Pynn is supported by corbels that feature a small checkerboard pattern. This decorative motif is used in various ways throughout the house to help achieve the Arts and Crafts goal of design unity.

Voysey's preferred material for furniture was oak. Strong, dense, heavy, with its texture of feathered grain, oak became the wood most closely associated with Arts and Crafts furniture in Britain and North America. Oak was the material of the medieval cabinet maker and the stuff of victorious galleons.

Gustav Stickley promoted his favored quarter-sawn American white oak as "strong fibered and sturdy," a reflection of the robust morality of the American people. Like Frank Lloyd Wright, Stickley believed wood should be cut in straight lines in order to emphasize its grain, which he liked to see rubbed to a ruddy glow with a thin layer of wax or coat of shellac. The choice of a material

appropriate for its purpose, natural, undisguised, and ideally indigenous, was of equal concern for Arts and Crafts architects. Philip Webb quarried sandstone for Standen in Sussex on site and incorporated in his design features of traditional local architecture, such as tile-hanging and oak weatherboarding. E.S. Prior decorated the façade of his eccentric Norfolk masterpiece, Home Place, with a knobbly pattern of local flint and brick. Charles Greene, of Greene and Greene, would search ravines for the perfect boulder for a wall or staircase. The belief that a house should be

ABOVE Stained glass was a key decorative element in the Arts and Crafts house on both sides of the Atlantic. The early figurative work of Morris & Co. was gradually superseded by more abstract designs. This window next to the front door of a new house was designed by the stained-glass artist Jeff Grainger.

bonded with its landscape both structurally and stylistically—was the cornerstone of what came to be known as "organic" architecture.

Generally, Arts and Crafts designers turned away from ostentatious materials, however natural. So wool, cotton, and linen were preferred over silk damask and velvet for curtains, upholsteries, and hangings; copper, brass, and iron over gilt or silver plate; pebbles, semiprecious stones, and enamel over precious stones. Morris wanted beauty to be available to all, and he inspired many other designers with his socialist ideals. But, like the

deceptive antimaterialism of today's minimalist interiors, the simplicity and quality of genuinely handmade Arts and Crafts products remained, in Morris's words, the "swinish luxury of the rich."

American Arts and Crafts interiors tend to be dominated by wood and its many shades, from pale honey to dark chocolate. American oak, gum wood, chestnut, and redwood were used for flooring, paneling, and extensively for built-in furniture. Walls between woodwork were sometimes white, but equally likely to have been painted a "cheerful . . . buff, brown and red, or occasionally deep blue

ABOVE LEFT AND RIGHT
The stylized leaf and flower shapes that form the pattern of glass in the front door of a modern home are inspired by the designs of Frank Lloyd Wright, who attributed his mastery at tessellating straight-edged shapes to a childhood passion for playing with wooden building bricks.

or rich green," as suggested by Charles Keeler, a devotee of William Morris, in his popular book *The Simple Home* (1904). Bedrooms were often papered in busy, intricate Morris designs which came in choice of colour combinations; the paler would have been considered most appropriate for these more private and "feminine" rooms.

In the U.S. the extensive use of white paint in interiors was associated with Federal and Colonial architecture, but in England it was the hallmark of the Arts and Crafts interior, and crucial to its effect. William Morris's daughter May Morris described

THE DRIVE TO REDUCE PATTERNS BASED ON NATURAL FORMS TO "THE UTMOST FLATNESS" WAS THE BEGINNINGS OF PURE ABSTRACTION.

how their drawing room "over the shop" in London's Queen Square was "made to shine with whitewash and white paint" as a backdrop for the rich, bright greens, blues, and reds of the embroideries and tapestries made by Morris & Co.

The contrast between areas of flat paint in shades of white and cream and the deep, warm colors of patterned textiles is one of the most distinctive decorative effects of the English Arts and Crafts interior. The drawing room at Standen, a house designed by Philip Webb and furnished with Morris & Co. textiles

and carpets, is an example of how pleasing this balance can be. Voysey described his ideal interior as "a well-proportioned room, with white-washed walls, plain carpet and simple oak furniture," the only ornament "a simple vase of flowers."

When Voysey did use color, he liked clear and vivid tones—green tiles surrounding a fireplace contrasted with red curtains, for example—dismissing the fashionable sepias and sludgy greens of the 1860s and 1870s as "mud and mourning." Edwin Lutyens, who was also a devotee of white paint, was

even more theatrical with color, reveling in the drama of snowy
woodwork framing black walls with a bold dash of yellow curtains
in his own London drawing room.

Between about 1880 and 1910, there was a gradual lightening
of color schemes which coincided with—and was probably
encouraged by—the introduction of electric lighting and the
incandescent gas mantle. Not only were both much brighter
than the oil or gas lamps they replaced, they were also much
cleaner. Today the greatest threats to our white walls and pale
upholstery are sticky fingers and muddy dogs' paws. We may
complain about pollution, but at least we don't have to put
gauze screens over our windows to catch the flakes of soot.

More than a century after William Morris's death, patterns by
him are still so ubiquitous that it is hard to suppress a small
visual groan at the sight of yet another box of tissues, bath hat,
stationery set, pencil case, or notebook embellished with his
instantly recognizable swirling acanthus leaves or stylized
sunflowers. Morris designs have become a visual commonplace,
victims of their own success. Over the years terrible liberties
have been taken with his original colors, most notably in
the 1970s when brown and orange versions of Morris fabrics
seemed to deck a million or more British living rooms.

Morris began designing wallpaper just a year after he launched
his decorating firm. His first attempt was "Trellis." Inspired by

the view of the garden from his upstairs study in Red House, it is a pattern of roses rambling over the wood-grained grid of a trellis complete with nails. Dotted among the roses are birds, drawn by Philip Webb. Although it is taken straight from nature, the pattern is essentially flat, as if flowers, leaves, and woodwork have been heavily ironed.

"Trellis" conforms perfectly to the Arts and Crafts ideal of taking inspiration from nature and transforming it by a process of simplification to make a repeating design that would not "jump out" from the wall, or indeed the sofa.

Both Morris and the architect Voysey, who was also a master of pattern, believed in the subservient role of wallpaper in a room. For Morris, wallpaper was "a makeshift," an inferior substitute for the textural richness of woven tapestry hangings or embroideries. Voysey was more scathing: "A wallpaper is of course only a background, and were your furniture good in form and colour, a very simple or quite undecorated treatment of the walls would be preferable." On the other hand, "elaborate papers of many colours" could help to disguise the "ugliness [of] most modern furniture."

The transformation of the three-dimensional into a stylized web of line and color that could be block- or roller-printed onto fabric or wallpaper, or traced onto fabric for embroidery, was key to the Arts and Crafts style. Morris based his designs almost exclusively on plant life, as their titles suggest: Honeysuckle, Daisy, Acanthus, Pomegranate. Other designers were more adventurous. Voysey, it seems, could extract an undulating, rhythmical repeat from almost anything, whether it was a nursery song or a sailing boat, a seahorse or a flame-licking demon. Herbert Horne crisscrossed trumpet-blowing angels on one of his fabrics for the Century Guild.

Voysey recommended reducing forms "to mere symbols," and evolved a highly personal system of symbolic motifs. Best known is the heart, which became his trademark, used as cutouts in furniture, as metal plates surrounding mailslots, and as embellishment for hinges. Voysey's was a particularly intricate visual code, but all Arts and Crafts designers used symbolism when devising patterns, in particular with reference to nature.

The Arts and Crafts drive to reduce patterns based on natural forms to Voysey's ideal of "the utmost flatness" was taken a step farther by later designers, and was the beginnings of pure abstraction. By 1900, Charles Rennie Mackintosh had distilled the rose down to a few, almost mathematical curves, while Frank Lloyd Wright's concrete hollyhocks, which give their name to his famous house of 1917, are virtually unrecognizable, such is the starkness of their geometry.

OPPOSITE, TOP TO BOTTOM The curvy, white-painted banisters in Sheila Scholes's Arts and Crafts house have a Swedish simplicity. A strong practical streak led Voysey to use the bird and berry design in several of his houses as a ventilation grille to improve the efficiency of the open fire. The same design makes stylish stationery.

THIS PAGE Like Frank Lloyd Wright, Charles Rennie Mackintosh took natural forms several steps closer to pure abstraction. The carved furniture, stenciled walls, and appliquéd curtains in Paul Morgan's Mackintosh bedroom feature some of the architect's favorite decorative motifs, such as the rose and the checkerboard.

OPPOSITE Much of the furniture in this Greene and Greene house is antique, yet the effect is far from old-fashioned, thanks to the straight lines and lack of frills of Craftsman designs.

THIS PAGE Arts and Crafts simplicity in a living room, a hall, and a bathroom is mixed with pieces from other eras and cultures for a look that is comfortable and contemporary.

WITH THEIR SOLIDITY AND CLEAN LINES, ARTS AND CRAFTS PIECES SEEM QUITE AT HOME IN THE 21ST-CENTURY INTERIOR.

RATIONAL AND PLAIN
furniture

Twenty-five years ago you could buy a good piece of Arts and Crafts furniture for pocket change. To do the same today you would need very large pockets. Arts and Crafts furniture is desirable, chic, and—if it can be attributed to one of the big names—expensive.

Fortunately for the modern collector, the big names inspired a following of lesser makers and manufacturers whose copycat designs are far more accessible. Lines of Arts and Crafts-style furniture labeled "the Quaint style"

ABOVE AND ABOVE RIGHT Antique furniture in Arts and Crafts style is solid, unpretentious and, above all, usable.

LEFT The oak hanging cabinet was designed for Little Thakeham by Sir Edwin Lutyens, the house's architect.

OPPOSITE Oak chairs at Little Thakeham flank an oak kneehole desk that has been decorated with panels of embossed copper.

or "New Art" were marketed by many leading furniture retailers. Both Liberty and Heal's sold copies of Morris & Co.'s popular "Sussex" chair, ready-to-wear versions of the catwalk original.

Arts and Crafts furniture is more than just fashionable; it is also eminently usable. An Arts and Crafts dining chair with a rush or padded leather seat and a high straight back is comfortable to sit in and sturdy enough to endure the rigors of family dining. An Arts and Crafts dining table won't wobble on spindly legs or worry with a high polish vulnerable to water stains and marks from sticky fingers. A Stickley drawer doesn't sag; a Voysey handle doesn't snag. The best Arts and Crafts furniture has a beauty that combines plain common sense with aesthetic conviction. The rational and relatively plain appearance of most Arts and Crafts furniture is a result of a concerted effort by a series of Victorian design reformers to simplify and clarify the confusion of styles that filled most people's houses. William Morris and Rossetti are both quoted as suggesting bonfires as the most expedient way to rid wealthy houses of the "unutterable rubbish" that filled them. Arson being unacceptable, persuasion had to suffice.

Books containing advice on interior decoration were increasingly popular in the second half of the 19th century. One of the first to promote the Arts and Crafts aesthetic was a book by Charles Eastlake, a designer and writer, published in 1868. Innocuously entitled *Hints on Household Taste in Furniture, Upholstery and other Details*, it strongly criticizes furnishings such as the contemporary settee or couch with its "general puffy and blown-out

IF YOU ASPIRED TO THE PHILOSOPHY BUT
COULDN'T AFFORD THE LOOK, AN ALTERNATIVE
WAS TO BUY FURNITURE FROM ONE OF THE
COMMERCIALLY PRODUCED LINES.

RIGHT In the music room of Greene and Greene's Duncan-Irwin House, a row of casement windows overlooks an inner courtyard. With its high pitched ceiling, exposed brickwork and rugged furniture, this room seems to prefigure today's loft conversions.

appearance" and promotes instead the rugged simplicity of furniture designed on the medieval model. Eastlake's book was influential and popular, running to seven editions in the U.S. Fourteen years later, in *The Decoration and Furnishing of Town Houses*, Colonel Robert Edis wrote: "Why cannot people understand that good taste and simplicity go hand in hand with common sense?"

As late as 1906 the Arts and Crafts architect M.H. Baillie Scott was ridiculing the typical suburban householder "pushed into a corner by insistent and triumphant furniture." Mainstream middle-class taste—that of the "ordinary" as opposed to the "cultured cottager" of Osbert Lancaster's satire—continued to prefer cheap ostentation to expensive restraint.

In a lecture of 1882, William Morris summed up his idea of "good citizen's furniture" as being "solid and well made in workmanship," adding that in its design it "should have nothing about it that is

not easily defensible, no monstrosities or extravagances, not even of beauty, lest we weary of it." Twenty years later, in Stickley's catalog of 1901, his definition of Arts and Crafts principles listed "the ideals of honesty of materials, solidity of construction, utility, adaptability to place, and aesthetic effect."

In practice, some of these "rules" were sidestepped. For example, Voysey strayed from the Arts and Crafts ideal of native materials by using Austrian oak because he preferred its straight grain. Greene and Greene employed exquisite ebony pegs to hide the screws that held their furniture together, making a minor mockery of the principle of "honest" construction.

Prominent, elongated hinges, which became a hallmark of the Arts and Crafts style, were an exhibition of "solidity of construction" with no real structural use—nobody could argue that strap hinges stretching the width of a door were crucial to the strength of a sideboard.

WHITE WALLS, BARE BOARDS, AND BEAUTIFULLY CRAFTED FURNISHINGS—WOODEN SETTLES, PLAIN HUTCHES, CHESTS, AND ARMOIRES—MAKE INTERIORS THAT ARE SERENE AND TIMELESS.

William Morris had strong opinions about furniture, but little interest in designing it. Early pieces by Morris & Co. are usually of oak, stained black or decorated with gesso and oil paint. While all flat patterns produced by Morris & Co., whether for fabrics, wallpapers, or carpets, share a recognizable style, the furniture ranges from the rush-seated austerity of the Sussex chair to the pomp of enormous Gothic cabinets designed by Philip Webb and richly decorated with Pre-Raphaelite figures. Later, when George Jack took over the company's furniture workshop

as chief designer, Morris & Co. furniture was closely based on Georgian designs, catering for the fashionable "Queen Anne revival" and sold as "of highest Sheraton finish" or "Chippendale style"—what today we would call reproduction.

Although we tend to think of Arts and Crafts furniture as strictly plain, some of it, even pieces by purists like Voysey, was quite elaborate. Morris distinguished between what he called "work-a-day" furniture—chairs, dining and working tables—and "state" furniture—cabinets and sideboards made "as much for

OPPOSITE, ABOVE
The Arts and Crafts
sideboard remains an
eminently practical
piece in today's hall or
living room. Its surface,
originally designed to
be the right height for
carving meat, is now
more likely to be used
to display ornaments.
Metal strap hinges are
typical of the way Arts
and Crafts design turned
elements of construction
to decorative effect.

OPPOSITE, BELOW A
Stickley oak armoire
with butterfly joints and
a Craftsman spindle
chair grace the bedroom
of a new house in the
Idaho mountains. The
ceiling beams use both
traditional and modern
woodwork techniques in
a house that effortlessly
blends old and new.

LEFT Interior decorator
Anthony Collett mixes
his own designs and Arts
and Crafts pieces with
panache in his London
home. His combined
bathroom and dressing
room is presided over by
an impressive Liberty
oak armoire with canted
sides and forged iron
banding. The doors are
secured with sliding
poles that double as
clothes and towel rods.

LEFT An original Arts and Crafts coat and hat stand—which, unlike lesser versions, doesn't wobble—makes an attractive freestanding bathroom towel rack.

RIGHT This English Arts and Crafts house retains all its original fireplaces, paneling, and built-in furniture. Built-in settles flanking the fireplace in the main bedroom are graceful and finely proportioned.

beauty's sake as for use." Voysey's designs for furniture, which represent the acme of Arts and Crafts discipline and refinement, fall readily into these categories. His dining chairs in unpolished oak are pared down to the essentials of legs, stretchers, and splats, their straight lines elongated to slim elegance, perhaps with a modest heart cutout as the only concession to ornament. By contrast, a piece of "state furniture" such as Voysey's Kelmscott "Chaucer" cabinet is an extravagant show-off. Made to hold Morris's masterpiece of printing, its body is plain while its doors are emblazoned with ostentatiously decorative brass hinges and plaques bearing cutout lettering backed with red suede.

Other leading designers and makers such as C.R. Ashbee could also produce work of puritan austerity alongside more glamorous pieces designed to stretch the skills of his craftsmen. Ashbee's Guild of Handicrafts made plain furniture, advertised in catalogs and similar in price and style to the Arts and Crafts lines sold by Liberty and Heal's in London, but Ashbee also designed splendid one-off pieces incorporating decorative metalwork, carving, embossed leather, and bands of inlay. As Walter Crane said of the Arts and Crafts style: "You might be almost plain enough to

please Thoreau, with a rush-bottomed chair, piece of matting, and oaken trestle table; or you might have gold and luster (the choice ware of William De Morgan) gleaming from the sideboard"—the Movement's aesthetic could embrace both "simplicity and splendour."

Old photographs of original Arts and Crafts interiors illustrate the difference. Ernest and Sidney Barnsley, both architects turned furniture designers who left London to establish workshops in the Cotswolds, created rooms in their country houses that verge on

TYPICAL OF THE STYLE OF BUILT-IN FURNITURE WERE HIGH-BACKED SETTLES SET INTO INGLENOOKS OR AROUND WIDE FIREPLACES.

minimalism. White walls, bare boards, and their own beautifully crafted furnishings—ladderback chairs, wooden settles, plain hutches—make interiors that are serene and timeless. In contrast, a photograph of the interior of May Morris's London house shows a room that is positively busy, with floor-to-cornice Willow wallpaper, close-packed pictures, and a couch with richly embroidered covers and cushions.

The set of beliefs uniting the different threads of Arts and Crafts style included the widely held conviction that a designer should be intimately involved in the process of creation. Few Arts and Crafts furniture makers actually wielded saws and planes, but all aspired to a thorough working knowledge of their materials and the techniques they demanded before putting pen to paper. Some designers were prepared to give the craftsmen who translated their drawings into three dimensions some latitude, following John Ruskin's ideal of the creative artisan. Others, like Voysey, having found workshops that could produce carpentry to a high enough standard, provided meticulous drawings and measurements to make sure their designs were executed precisely as intended.

ABOVE This white-painted reproduction of a Mackintosh chair owes a debt to Arts and Crafts designers such as Voysey in its exaggeratedly high back, but is more glamorous and less robust than its plain wood precursors.

Toward the end of the 19th century, Arts and Crafts began to be recognized as a style of interior design as opposed to a set of high-falutin' ideals. Initially the clientele for the work of Arts and Crafts architects and designers had been extremely rarefied—a small group of like-minded artists and esthetes who bought from each other or were commissioned by wealthy patrons. Custom-made hand-crafted furniture was beyond the reach

of most people. If you aspired to the philosophy but couldn't afford the look, an alternative was to buy furniture from one of the commercially produced lines. Some of these, such as the line produced by Ashbee's Guild of Handicrafts, were true in both style and construction to the Arts and Crafts ethos. A few prettified the simple, country-cottage designs of purists like Sidney Barnsley or Ernest Gimson to come up with versions verging on the

ABOVE Unnamed and unattributed, the chairs in Mark Kirkley's living room in Sussex, England, are all versions of the so-called "Morris" chair, bought cheaply at auction and re-upholstered in fresh modern white muslin.

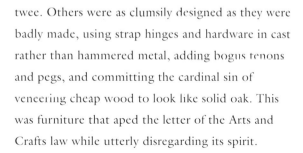

twee. Others were as clumsily designed as they were badly made, using strap hinges and hardware in cast rather than hammered metal, adding bogus tenons and pegs, and committing the cardinal sin of veneering cheap wood to look like solid oak. This was furniture that aped the letter of the Arts and Crafts law while utterly disregarding its spirit.

In the field of furniture design, Ambrose Heal and Gustav Stickley were notable exceptions to the theory that Arts and Crafts ideals could not be converted into accessible products. Heal joined the

THIS PAGE Simple cut-outs and restrained inlays decorate these very different Arts and Crafts chairs, one faintly Gothic, one almost Swiss (above), and all sharing a common design preference for straight lines and flat surfaces.

LEFT The sturdy country style of Arts and Crafts chairs is easily reinterpreted to make low, comfortable rockers. This unsigned "mission" rocking chair is similar to versions made by Stickley.

BELOW LEFT Arts and Crafts armchairs often had adjustable backs, making up for lack of springs and padded upholstery with deep seats and supportive back rests. White cotton coverings and cushions link the armchairs in this living room, each a variation on this popular Arts and Crafts design.

RIGHT The lines between old and new are carefully blurred in this 1919 Craftsman bungalow, where a modern dining table and chairs sit on a rug designed by Archibald Knox, and new, craftsman-made glass-fronted cabinets hold a collection of period glass, china, and pottery.

FAR RIGHT, ABOVE AND BELOW Unusual low-backed Arts and Crafts chairs in a dining room and a kitchen look decidedly modern. Reproduction furniture (top right) makes an informal dining area.

family firm in 1893 and began to design simple, solid oak furniture, which first appeared in the company's catalog in 1897. While clearly influenced by the work and writings of Morris, Lethaby, Gimson, and other leaders of the Arts and Crafts movement, Heal had a commercial background that meant his designs were cleverly marketed and attractively priced.

In 1899 Heal's catalog boasted: "Whilst taking advantage of all that is best in machinery, we have been careful not to allow the taint of the usual trade machine furniture to invade the workshop. We are in fact most careful to give free expression to that individual craftsmanship . . . without which no cabinet work . . . can hope to be in any real sense—artistic."

Gustav Stickley was similarly pragmatic, as well as being a genuine idealist and a skilled designer. His magazine, *The Craftsman*, was the perfect means by which to market the lifestyle he believed

INTEREST IN PREINDUSTRIAL SKILLS AND WORKMANSHIP STIMULATED A TRADE IN ANTIQUE FURNITURE, ESPECIALLY OF THE SIMPLE, COUNTRY-MADE VARIETY.

THIS PAGE This oak table by Liberty is a perfect example of the style crossover between English Arts and Crafts and that curvaceous foreign import, Art Nouveau. Liberty often made a success of marrying the two styles.

OPPOSITE, LEFT Seen in situ at Little Thakeham, the same table with its Art Nouveau cutouts and Arts and Crafts tenon joints sits next to an early 20th-century oak chair, the style of which is similarly difficult to categorize.

in and to promote sales of his furnishings. The first three issues were devoted to, respectively, Morris, Ruskin, and the medieval guilds. Having given full vent to his idealism, Stickley proceeded to use a combination of craftsmanship and the latest machinery and to make "oak furniture that shows plainly what it is, and in which the design and construction harmonize with the wood."

Frank Lloyd Wright was equally comfortable with machinery, pointing out in his lecture of 1901: "The machine . . . has made it possible to so use [wood] without waste that the poor as well as the rich may enjoy today beautiful surface treatments of clean, strong forms." To this extent the American Arts and Crafts movement achieved a level of democracy that William Morris only dreamed of. As Stickley put it: "As we have no monarchs and no aristocracy the life of the plain people is the life of the

ABOVE AND TOP
Unpretentious pieces such as these side tables, neither of great age or value, slip seamlessly into the modern Arts and Crafts interior.

ABOVE RIGHT AND RIGHT Mark Kirkley mixes modern pieces with good-quality unattributed antiques such as the circular oak table with its hammered copper top and heart cutouts

nation." "Plain people" could afford to buy Stickley furniture—and they could also afford to build a modest Craftsman house to put it in, from plans published in *The Craftsman*. With its strong vertical lines of splat and spindle, Stickley's furniture is as distinctive as Voysey's. And, although Stickley was no architect, he shared Voysey's commitment to creating integrated interiors, filling his magazine with attractive color drawings of fully furnished rooms as well as elevations and plans for houses.

The desire to control the whole look of an interior was shared by most of the great Arts and Crafts designers, many of whom trained as architects. Inspired by the multitalented Morris, who had also begun his working life apprenticed to an architect, they

RIGHT AND BELOW
Arts and Crafts put the wooden bedstead back in vogue after the predominance of metal, which had been thought more hygienic and less prone to harbor bugs. Today's Craftsman-style bedroom favors reproduction wooden bedsteads because antique double beds, such as those shown, tend to be too narrow to suit our modern ideas of comfort.

THE BEST ARTS AND CRAFTS FURNITURE HAS A BEAUTY THAT COMBINES PLAIN COMMON SENSE WITH AESTHETIC CONVICTION.

readily turned their attentions to other branches of domestic design, including fabrics, wallpapers, and metalwork, as well as furniture. Architects such as Voysey, Greene and Greene, Baillie Scott, and Wright had opportunities to build and furnish houses, and apply themselves to every last detail of their interiors, from curtain color to window latches, from bathroom tiles to drawing-room rugs.

One way to maximize control over the furnishings in a house was to incorporate as much built-in furniture as possible. Built-in furniture became a feature of the Arts and Crafts interior, and not just closets and dressers for bedrooms or cabinets for kitchens. Even more typical

of the style are built-in sideboards or hutches in dining rooms, deep seats in bay windows, and high-backed settles built into inglenooks or around wide fireplaces. Wooden screens were often used to create rooms within rooms: "cozy corners" for a private conversation or a quiet read.

Writing about old houses, the Arts and Crafts architect E.S. Prior praised "that architectural amalgam which blended the structure with its contents, the screens and panelling which, half room, half furniture, cemented one to the other." Quite apart from the fact that it accorded with the Arts and Crafts ideal of integration, built in furniture also appealed to the late Victorian obsession with hygiene. Built-in furniture was largely an Arts and Crafts innovation. Another was a fashion for antiques. The interest in preindustrial skills and workmanship stimulated a trade in antique furniture, especially of the simple, country-made variety. The effect was significantly to reduce the demand for brand-new furnishings and encourage the combining of old and new. Arts and Crafts furniture can look surprisingly modern and perfectly at home in a 21st-century interior. Its typically clean lines are compatible with most styles of contemporary furniture, while its solid, traditional construction and craftsmanship provide more intangible pleasures.

THIS PAGE Straight narrow spindles finished with small curved corbels were used for Craftsman chairs and settles as well as for beds. This reproduction double bed looks appealingly sturdy and capacious.

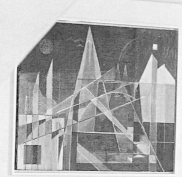

WILLIAM MORRIS BELIEVED THAT A PIECE OF
POTTERY SHOULD SHOW THE NATURE OF THE
CLAY AND REVEAL THE HAND OF THE POTTER.

LUSTROUS AND COLORFUL

ceramics
and glassware

**THIS PAGE AND
OPPOSITE, ABOVE** A
modern pot by Ray West
emphasizes the oriental
simplicity of a 1917
Craftsman interior. The
pot's experimental glaze
and sinuous applied
decoration contrast with
the straight lines and
dark wood of its setting.

OPPOSITE, BELOW
Curvaceous modern
pottery is again used
as a foil for the boldly
rectilinear designs that
surround it.

When Morris & Co. showed its stained glass in the 1862
Exhibition at South Kensington, it was so perfect an imitation
of medieval examples that many thought the firm must have
used old glass. Stained-glass windows, mainly for churches, were
initially its bread and butter. Designed by Edward Burne-Jones,
Ford Madox Brown, and Dante Gabriel Rossetti, as well as
by Morris himself, major commissions included windows for
St. Michael's, Brighton, and Jesus College Chapel, Cambridge.

Figurative stained glass was a vital component of the medieval
aesthetic admired by Morris and his circle, but its strong religious
overtones did not easily transfer to a household setting. Early
commissions from Morris & Co. for secular stained glass replaced
religious themes with scenes from Arthurian legend. Later in the
century, Arts and Crafts stained glass embraced more homebound
subjects—idyllic landscapes, trees and stylized flowers—better
suited to front doors and drawing-room windows.

Among the finest examples of Arts and Crafts stained glass is
the work of Emil Lange for the architects Greene and Greene. In
the Gamble House an oak tree in shades of green and amber
spreads its branches across the entrance to the house, filling the
hall with a golden glow in daylight. Glass lamps and lanterns in

ABOVE AND LEFT Early 20th-century Royal Lancastrian pottery by Pilkington in vibrant blues and oranges is grouped on a quarry-tiled window ledge at Little Thakeham. The simple forms and lack of decoration of all these pots concentrate attention on the quality of the glaze, its depth, texture, and color.

OPPOSITE Plain pots and pretty flowers make a striking composition on the table in Anthony Collett's dining room.

the same sunny shades echo the design in simplified form. Internal doors are inset with panels of colored glass, and windows over the dining-room sideboard depict a stylized blossoming vine. Throughout the house, light is filtered and warmed by its passage through stained glass.

Frank Lloyd Wright took the plant forms of Greene and Greene several steps farther toward abstraction with art-glass designs that reduced an ear of wheat to a stack of slim parallelograms, and a tree of life to columns of squares. This delicate geometry of leaded plain glass with touches of color that patterns the windows of many of Wright's early houses has been endlessly imitated, and used for lampshades and kitchen-cabinet doors as well as windows.

There is no readily identifiable Arts and Crafts style of table glass. May Morris, in her evocative description of her father's drawing room at Kelmscott House in London, recalls "the discreet glimmer of old glass" in cabinets, and even new glass, such as that designed by Philip Webb for Red House, and later sold by Morris & Co., looks very much like antique glass, being closely based on German and Venetian glass from the 17th and 18th centuries. There was a preference for the handblown and simple over the molded or lavishly cut.

ORIENTAL ART EMBODIED MANY OF THE QUALITIES THAT ARTS AND CRAFTS SOUGHT TO PROMOTE: UNITY, SIMPLICITY, HARMONY, AND A REVERENCE FOR THE NATURAL WORLD.

Pottery was a different matter. Cheap, mass-produced china, factory-made and transfer-printed, flooded the market in the late 19th century. Pottery was a craft that William Morris did not master, but he still had strong opinions on the subject, believing that a piece of pottery should show the nature of the clay and reveal the hand of the potter. The fine Sèvres and Dresden china in the display cabinets of opulent Victorian drawing rooms was rejected as over-sophisticated. Far more in

tune with Arts and Crafts style was the blue-and-white Nanking and Delft that Rossetti had a passion for. Set against a deep sea green, as in the dining room at Standen, blue-and-white Chinese porcelain was the epitome of late Victorian "artistic" taste.

Unlike weaving, stained glass, or even metalwork, pottery required the amenities of a factory for the final stages of firing. Small-scale kilns were not developed until the 1920s. One way around this was to use factory blanks. Some of the most

ABOVE A collection of dark metallic Dicker ware makes a striking display on a small oak hutch.

RIGHT The panel is in the style of the American ceramicist Ernest Batchelder, while the matt tiles recall the plain Grueby tiles that Stickley favored.

charming hand-painted Arts and Crafts pottery—for example, the work of Alfred and Louise Powell—was painted freehand underglaze on pieces supplied by the large manufacturers.

Even William De Morgan, one of the most celebrated British Arts and Crafts potters, who made a specialty of shimmering luster glazes, initially used mass-produced tiles as the canvas for his handpainted decoration. After a

ABOVE, FAR RIGHT Timeless forms with singular glazes again show the influence of oriental ceramics.

BELOW, FAR RIGHT A collection of green Barnstaple pottery mixed in with French and Belgian pots of similar style is displayed on Mark Kirkley's oak shelves.

disastrous attempt to fire kilns connected to an ordinary household chimney—which promptly set fire to the roof—he moved to premises in Chelsea and built a proper kiln, where he also started to make his own clays. Tiles and pots by De Morgan, featuring sunflowers, birds, fishes, sailing ships, and mythical beasts, were sold by Morris & Co., their gleaming all-over patterns combining richness and restraint, and complementing Morris's own designs for fabrics and wallpapers.

Some of the large potteries, such as Doulton, responded to the vogue for "Art" pottery by setting up smaller workshops within their factories where designers and decorators could have more

freedom to produce studio pottery. Minton developed a line of tiles in fashionable Moorish and Persian designs with a handmade feel. Pilkington employed Voysey, Lewis F. Day and Walter Crane, while Teco Art Pottery in the U.S. commissioned designs from Frank Lloyd Wright.

Plainer Arts and Crafts pottery was strongly influenced by Japanese and Chinese ceramics. Oriental art embodied many of the qualities that adherents of Arts and Crafts sought to promote: unity, simplicity, harmony, and a reverence for the natural world. Oriental glazes were much admired, and efforts were made by the Ruskin Pottery in Britain and Chelsea Keramic

ABOVE LEFT The vases with elongated necks on the mantelpiece in Anthony Collett's London dining room are Bermantoft pottery. They are part of a grouping worthy of a still life.

ABOVE A green pottery vase by Ray West (left) has been teamed with two modern art-glass vases by Lundberg Glass. The colors and shapes of this group are typical of original Arts and Crafts pieces.

THERE WAS AN ARTS AND CRAFTS PREFERENCE FOR THE HANDBLOWN AND SIMPLE OVER THE MOLDED OR LAVISHLY CUT.

Art Works in the U.S. to rediscover lost techniques such as the thick red glaze known as *sang de boeuf*. Grueby pottery, with its distinctive matt glazes in gentle greens and blues, was recommended by Gustav Stickley as appropriately chaste adornment for the Craftsman interior.

There was ample opportunity in the Arts and Crafts house to display the art of the potter— on the deep plate racks that topped wooden wall paneling or took the place of the picture rail; as tiles around a fireplace; as set pieces on the mantelpiece; or ranged on the built-in hutches that had been promoted from the kitchen to pride of place in the dining room. It might be gloriously decorated like a De Morgan platter or utterly plain, but to deserve its place it should fulfill Morris's advice to pottery students and have "qualities besides those which made it for ordinary use."

ABOVE LEFT A collection of Hoffman glass adorns a living-room wall. Its sunny tinge is picked up in the glow of the metal lamp built under the shelf. A co-founder of the Wiener Werkstätte, Joseph Hoffman was inspired by the Arts and Crafts movement.

ABOVE On the same shelving is a glass bowl by Kolo Moser. The slight irregularity of shape marks it out as a handblown piece.

LEFT True to Arts and Crafts ideals, the original brass canopy is clearly handmade, probably by a local blacksmith, and makes a decorative virtue of its rows of metal rivets and the light-reflecting qualities of its uneven surface.

RIGHT This 1940s house in California includes original Craftsman-inspired metalwork such as the repoussé copper paneling that partially surrounds a bedroom fireplace.

Arts and Crafts designers and theorists could be splendidly rude, especially when denouncing furnishings of which they did not approve. "Cold, clumsy and vulgar" is Ruskin's description of cast-iron decoration. "Depraved coarseness, brutality and sickly elaboration characterise the metalwork on nearly all modern furniture," ranted Voysey.

Metalware that was hand-crafted, or at least looked hand-crafted, was integral to Arts and Crafts architecture and furniture design. The emphasis on "honesty" gave details of construction such as hinges a new and important role. Instead of being "dishonestly" hidden or disguised, they were emphasized and exaggerated. One of William Morris's early furniture designs, for a settle and hutch now at Red House, extends decorative iron hinges across the whole width of the planked cabinet doors.

Elongated hinges in matt hammered metal became a trademark feature used by almost all Arts and Crafts architects and furniture makers as a stamp of their design integrity.

While mainstream Victorian furniture makers and architects were satisfied with standard lines of metal hardware, Arts and Crafts practitioners designed their own, finding individual blacksmiths or small manufacturers to make them. Voysey may have been excessively controlling in his view that "everything inside the house [is] within the architect's province from fittings and furniture to the very toothbrushes," but, toothbrushes aside, he was speaking for all true Arts and Crafts architects. Voysey is justly famous for his witty and original metal hardware, his heart-shaped mail boxes, and the swooping curves of his elegant

HONEST AND DEMOCRATIC
metalware

METALWARE THAT WAS HAND-CRAFTED, OR AT LEAST LOOKED HAND-CRAFTED, WAS INTEGRAL TO ARCHITECTURE AND FURNITURE DESIGN.

door latches. Window catches and door hardware by Lutyens in his "Old English" houses such as Little Thakeham are as beautiful to look at as they are satisfying to use. Philip Webb designed glorious repoussé cheeks for the fireplaces at Standen, hammered out in glossy mild steel to refract and reflect the firelight.

Generally, Arts and Crafts metalwork is matt rather than shiny. Favored metals were iron, copper, and brass—the mineral equivalents of indigenous woods such as oak and elm. Semiprecious stones and enameling were preferred both for

THE METALS FAVORED BY THE DESIGNERS WERE IRON, COPPER, AND BRASS—THE MINERAL EQUIVALENTS OF INDIGENOUS WOODS SUCH AS OAK AND ELM.

jewelry and for decorative household wares as being more "of the people" than precious gemstones. Typical of this type of "democratic" metalware are the plain wall plaques, salvers, and caskets produced in Gustav Stickley's metal workshops, originally established in 1902 to make the fresh-from-the-smithy style hardware essential to his furniture's rugged look.

Some designers excelled in silver, notably C.R. Ashbee, whose graceful, fluid pieces are frequently described as "Art Nouveau" even though Ashbee himself would have rejected the label.

DETAILS OF CONSTRUCTION SUCH AS HINGES AND LATCHES TOOK ON A NEW IMPORTANCE.

Another exceptional designer of silverware often put under the Arts and Crafts umbrella is Christopher Dresser. Famed for the extreme modernity of his style, which is simple to the point of minimalism, Dresser in fact supported machine manufacture, and wrote a book refuting many of Ruskin's most dearly held ideals.

Predictably, the Arts and Crafts reverence for the craftsman made was commercially exploited. Liberty's lines of Arts and Crafts metalware, Cymric and Tudric, were a huge success. Almost entirely machine-made to designs by Archibald Knox, they were dye-stamped complete with bogus hammer marks. The effect is entirely convincing to modern eyes, schooled in the uniformity of mass-produced perfection, but it is not hard to understand why Ashbee scathingly referred to this fashionable department store as "Messrs. Nobody, Novelty and Co."

**THIS PICTURE AND
ABOVE RIGHT** The metal
chains and fixtures of
these lights are original,
but the art-glass shades
are new, handblown to a
pattern known as zipper.
Glass was invariably
used to cloak the
newfangled light bulb
in the Craftsman home.

BELOW LEFT AND RIGHT
Lighting is often the
most obvious decorative
feature of otherwise
sober Arts and Crafts
interiors. The feminine
curves of this lily-pad
table lamp with its
pretty glass shades add a
touch of frivolity to the
bedroom of a Greene
and Greene house.

FROM SIMPLE BRASS CANDLE SCONCES TO ELABORATE
LAMPS WITH PARCHMENT SHADES, ARTS AND CRAFTS
LIGHTING ADDS PANACHE TO TODAY'S INTERIOR.

EXCITING INNOVATIONS IN
lighting

The Arts and Crafts period saw the start
of a revolution in home lighting and a
move away from the murky yellow flare
of gaslight that had dominated the
19th century. The occasional power
outage or candlelit soirée reminds us
how shadowy and romantic our rooms
look without electricity, but generally
we are used to a level of illumination
that would have been quite alien to the
average Victorian householder.

A common Victorian reaction to the
first electric-light bulbs was one of slight
horror—the light they produced was
too bright, while electricity itself was
not only invisible, but, unlike gas, also
completely without odor. How would
you know if it was leaking out?

Although by the early 1890s a
few local suppliers were generating
electricity for sale in big cities, it
remained too expensive for most
consumers, too mysterious for others.

However, the incandescent gas mantle, another late-Victorian innovation, also produced a brighter, cleaner light, and was more widely accepted because it could be adapted to work with the existing piped gas supply. While public buildings and grander houses were gradually being converted to electric lighting, more ordinary houses were brighter, too. Apart from the lighting that was piped or wired into a house, there was additional lighting in the form of portable oil and kerosene lamps and the ever-useful candle.

Arts and Crafts designers in glass and metal applied themselves to the design of all these types of light fixture, from simple brass candle sconces to elaborate table lamps with beaten metal or parchment shades. Architects, often building from scratch and concerned to incorporate modern conveniences in their designs, embraced electricity and were responsible for some of the most attractive early electric-light fixtures. Thick pleated-silk

ABOVE LEFT New lamps based on a Neideken-Wright design bathe the walls of an architect's hall in a golden light.

ABOVE The original metal-and-glass lantern lighting the narrow stairwell of the Duncan-Irwin House is perfectly proportioned to fit its position, and it echoes the elongated wooden paneling on the walls.

LEFT The landing and stairs of this house, with its arched sash window, could almost be Queen Anne, but the hanging lantern is unmistakably Arts and Crafts.

FAR LEFT The lights for the great hall of this Arts and Crafts home were commissioned from a local designer-craftsman whose grandfather had once lived in the house.

THIS PICTURE This wall lamp by the modern craftsman Sam Mossaedi uses pegged wood as a frame for the glass shade in the style of lighting by Greene and Greene.

ABOVE RIGHT No Craftsman dining table was complete without its tailored hanging light that cast a bright pool, but did not dazzle the eyes of the diners.

RIGHT A lantern wall-light hangs in the beamed hall of a shingle house on New York's Fisher's Island.

THIS PAGE Frank Lloyd
Wright's Taliesin lamp is
more glow-in-the-dark
sculpture than usable
light. Meaning "shining
brow" in Welsh, Taliesin
is the name Wright gave
the house he built for
himself in Wisconsin—
the house for which the
light was originally
designed. This small
reproduction decorates
the master bedroom of a
1917 Craftsman house.

**OPPOSITE, CLOCKWISE
FROM TOP LEFT** This
simple and sophisticated
wooden floor lamp was
designed by Wright for
another of his homes,
Taliesin West.
A Wright reproduction
hangs above the stairs
in a Los Angeles house
dating from the 1960s.
Ever innovative, Wright
incorporated a reading
lamp in the extended
arm of a sofa seen here
in reproduction.
Set against windows
screened with stretched
fabric on plain wooden
frames, this Wright
reproduction in a 1940s
Los Angeles house has a
delicacy and refinement
typical of Japanese style.

shades were used to minimize the unfamiliar glare, especially for lights hanging over dining or billiard tables. Otherwise, opalescent glass shades elegantly cloaked the newfangled electric bulbs and their large filaments.

Concerned with every detail of their houses, architects such as Charles and Henry Greene designed electric light fixtures in wood and glass to match the wood and glass used elsewhere in the interiors, hanging them in order to define

ARCHITECTS WERE RESPONSIBLE FOR SOME OF THE MOST STYLISH EARLY LIGHT FIXTURES.

separate areas within a room by the pools of light they cast. Frank Lloyd Wright was similarly at pains to specify the precise placing of light fixtures in a room, even incorporating lights in wooden columns that formed part of a dining table.

In North America, the lantern, with a metal framework encasing glass, was popular in the Arts and Crafts home. Its rustic appeal was often emphasized by the forged iron chains from which it hung, sometimes in groups to form a type of rugged chandelier. Many variations on the Craftsman lantern are still being manufactured as light fixtures today. The most authentic are those that eschew shiny brass in favor of patinated matt finishes.

THE BOLD, FLAT, SIMPLIFIED TEXTILE DESIGNS
FAVORED BY ARTS AND CRAFTS TRANSLATE
PARTICULARLY WELL INTO A MODERN SETTING.

ENDURINGLY POPULAR
textiles

Fabric by the furlong was a dominant feature of the ordinary interior in late Victorian times. Windows were swagged and swathed in layers of it; pianos and tables were shrouded in it. Even fireplaces might have their own fringed valances and pairs of curtains—a bizarre decorative ploy advertised at the time as a means of "modernizing" a room economically. Favorite textiles for receiving rooms tended to be heavy, hairy, and ponderous, their claustrophobic effect heightened by their dark, rich colors.

By contrast, rooms designed by Arts and Crafts reformers were a breath of fresh air. Instead of thick folds of dust-catching serge, there were simple, unlined curtains in cotton chintz hanging from plain metal rods. A table might be decorated

RIGHT Craftsman pieces such as this reproduction settle can be transformed by the choice of upholstery fabric.

BELOW These printed cotton chintzes are from Morris & Co. The top one is a new design inspired by the style of William Morris; the other three are original Morris patterns.

with a pale linen runner rather than floor-scraping chenille. Instead of deeply buttoned velvet, block-printed cottons were used for upholstery.

William Morris, his ideas and designs, dominated Arts and Crafts textiles, and had a huge influence on textile design in general. In 1913, nearly twenty years after his death, the London *Times* noted: "Much of the present-day style of decorated fabrics is stamped with the personality of William Morris." Following in Morris's footsteps, a range of artists and architects, including C.F.A. Voysey,

OPPOSITE A Craftsman innovation was the table runner—a vestigial table cloth often embellished with simple appliquéd designs. This richly figured runner uses a modern fabric inspired by Celtic art.

RIGHT The design for this contemporary rug is based on an original by C.F.A. Voysey.

Lewis F. Day, and Walter Crane, turned their attentions to fabrics and wallpapers, producing patterns of great originality for a number of manufacturers and retailers. People who could not afford a hand-blocked chintz from Morris & Co., or a wool double cloth woven by Alexander Morton & Co. to a design by Voysey, could buy any number of cheaper imitations.

Today the genuine article would still command a premium. Sanderson holds nearly 100 original wood-blocks for Morris designs—works of art in themselves—from which it can, at a price, print wallpapers and fabrics to special commission. Cheaper versions of Morris designs are roller-printed and lack the depth and vibrancy of their hand-blocked superiors.

Morris's life-long love of textiles began with a passion for embroidery. Having taught himself the basic techniques, he proceeded to teach them to his wife, Janey, and her sister Elizabeth, so that they could work woolen hangings to his designs to drape the walls at Red House. The effect was rich and textural, medieval in spirit, but a far cry from the fuss and fustiness he and his followers were so

APPLIQUÉ WAS A POPULAR CRAFTSMAN EMBROIDERY TECHNIQUE, COMBINING AS IT DOES A CERTAIN NAIVETÉ WITH THE OPPORTUNITY FOR BOLD EFFECTS.

RIGHT Arts and Crafts rejected the overblown realism of mainstream late Victorian fabric and wallpaper design in favor of strong, often abstract patterns.

OPPOSITE, LEFT The abstract nature of many Craftsman designs gives them a very modern look. Linen was sought, as it is today, for its slightly rough, homespun qualities.

OPPOSITE, RIGHT These modern appliquéd pillows were inspired by Craftsman designs. Appliqué was a popular embroidery technique.

eager to avoid. Elevating embroidery to a minor art form became an Arts and Crafts campaign, and led to the founding in 1872 of The Royal School of Art Needlework. Newly created schools of art taught embroidery skills to keen amateurs. Many of the students were upper-middle-class women with time on their hands. Their work was often of superb quality, an example of home craftwork at its finest.

Workshops were set up all over Britain and the U.S. to revive the skills of embroidery. Ladies of leisure learned how to spin and weave, while others found a way to supplement the household income by working from home. In North America the traditional techniques of patchwork, netting, candlewick, and rag rug making were rediscovered.

It was in this way that Arts and Crafts textiles came closest to achieving William Morris's hopelessly unrealistic ambition to provide beauty

for the home that could be enjoyed by rich and poor alike. The not-so-rich for whom most handmade furnishings were impossibly expensive could indulge in an embroidery kit with a pattern by Morris marked on the cloth with threads included.

Morris designs were equally fashionable in the U.S., but they were even more expensive after 1890, when duties as high as 60 percent were imposed on imported textiles. The fabrics most commonly used in American Craftsman interiors are the home-produced woven linens and canvases championed by Gustav Stickley, who had established his Craftsman textile department in 1903. They were solid rather than patterned, in misty greens and blues. The canvas was a fairly coarse mix of jute and flax, while the "antique" linen achieved its homespun look with irregularly twisted yarn and a loose weave. The linen was thought particularly suitable for unlined curtains in a deep straw color that filtered daylight and gave the room a warm glow.

Like Morris, Gustav Stickley marketed embroidery designs as kits that could be made into curtains, table runners, and cushions. Embroidered on the same linen or canvas, Stickley's spare patterns, featuring his favored motifs of stylized ginkgo leaves, poppies, lotuses, and wild roses, look better suited to the amateur embroiderer than Morris's typically complex creations.

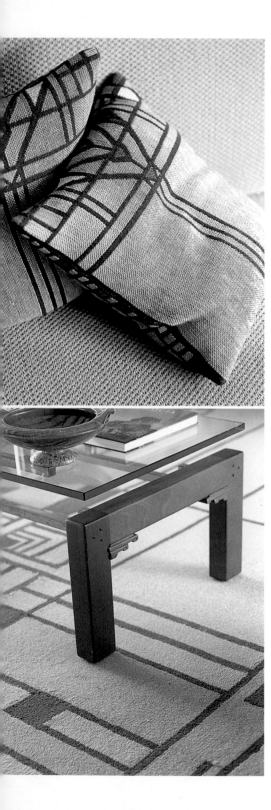

In the same way that machines had taken over the tasks of spinning, printing, and weaving, synthetic aniline dyes, derived from coal tar, had replaced traditional vegetable dyes.

Aniline dyes were cheap and cheerful, but purists such as William Morris had no liking for their garish colors, and disapproved of the fact that the colors rapidly faded. Morris conducted extensive experiments with natural dyes. For several years, while he was exploring the possibilities of woad, his hands were permanently stained blue.

In addition to printed cottons, Morris & Co. produced woven silks, woven wool, tapestry hangings, and carpets. The majority of the designs for these fabrics were the work of William Morris himself, although he usually deferred to the draftsmanship of others when he wanted to incorporate animals, birds, or figures

OPPOSITE, LEFT Like her craftsman forebears, Ann Chaves, the owner of the Duncan-Irwin House, has adorned its interior with examples of her own work, such as these beautiful embroidered pillows.

OPPOSITE, RIGHT The calm, well-spaced patterns applied to rugs and carpets, such as these by Archibald Knox, go well with modern furnishings.

THE TRADITIONAL TECHNIQUES OF PATCHWORK, NETTING, CANDLEWICK, AND RAG RUG MAKING WERE REDISCOVERED.

ABOVE LEFT These chic masculine pillows are based on a design by Frank Lloyd Wright. Many of Wright's original fabric designs are still made today, while still more are inspired by his endlessly inventive pattern-making for everything from stained glass to ceramic tiles.

LEFT This Liberty rug is a Wright design, its field crisscrossed by a typically spare grid of lines, squares, and rectangles.

into his designs. The famous tapestries that were produced by Morris & Co., woven on medieval-style high-warp looms at Merton Abbey, feature figures by Edward Burne-Jones.

The more opulent woven fabrics produced by Morris & Co. tend toward the grand, baronial end of the Arts and Crafts spectrum. Even these began with hands-on experiments by Morris, who taught himself how to weave cloth and tapestries and to hand-knot carpets before they were commercially produced by his company. At one stage he made and installed in his bedroom a handloom based on those he had seen in the homes of Icelandic farmers, opining with splendid arrogance: "If a chap can't compose an epic poem while he's weaving tapestry he had better shut up." Well known and respected in his day as a poet and a translator of Icelandic sagas, as well as a designer and campaigner, William Morris probably remains in a minority of one as someone who did manage to combine the two activities.

RESOURCES

GENERAL

The Arts & Crafts Society
1194 Bandera Drive
Ann Arbor, MI 48103
(734) 665 4729
www.arts-crafts.com
The society's website gives
sources for all types of Arts &
Crafts items, from ceramics to
building products.

AUCTION HOUSES

Butterfields Auctioneers
7601 Sunset Boulevard
Los Angeles, CA 90046
(323) 850 7500
www.butterfields.com

Christie's East
219 East 67th Street
New York, NY 10021
(212) 606 0400
www.christies.com

David Rago Arts & Crafts
17 South Main Street
Lambertville, NJ 08530
(609) 397 9374
www.ragoarts.com

Sotheby's
1334 York Avenue
New York, NY 10021
(212) 606 7000
www.sothebys.com

Toomey/Treadway
818 North Boulevard
Oak Park, IL 60301
(708) 383 5234
www.treadwaygallery.com

FURNITURE

American Furnishings Co.
1409 West Third Avenue
Columbus, OH 43212
(614) 488 7263
americanfurnishings.com
Reproduction Arts & Crafts
furniture, lighting, rugs,
pottery and glass.

The Antique Way
11729 Santa Monica Blvd
West Los Angeles, CA 90025
(310) 477 3971
Original and reproduction Arts
& Crafts and Mission Oak
furniture; restoration service.

Berman Gallery
136 N 2nd Street
Philadelphia, PA 19106
(215) 733 0707
bermangallery.com
Original and reproduction
furniture from the American
Arts & Crafts movement.

Brian Krueger
c/o Graham Lee Associates Inc.
2870 East 54th Street
Vernon, CA 90058
(323) 581 8203

Byer Woodworking
136 East St Joseph Street
Unit E
Arcadia, CA 91006
(626) 445 7451

The Cabinetmaker
1714 East Owl Hollow Road
Paoli, IN 47454
(812) 723 3461
www.the-cabinetmaker.com
Reproductions of Greene and
Greene furniture and other
designs from the American
Arts & Crafts movement.

Carol Grant Decorative Arts
510 South Washington
Royal Oak, MI 48067
248.398.1411
Mission furniture, art pottery;
lighting, and accessories.

Craftsman Antiques
16 Foxhill Rd.
Branchville, NJ 07826
(973) 455 8547
Arts & Crafts furniture,
pottery, metalwork, linens,
and lighting.

Craftsman Antiques
Telegraph Avenue
Oakland, CA 94609
(510) 595 7977
Arts & Crafts furniture, art
pottery, handwrought metal,
and lighting.

The Craftsman Home
3048 Claremont Avenue
Berkeley, CA 94705
(510) 655 6503
www.craftsmanhome.com
Arts & Crafts period and revival
home furnishings.

David Rago Arts & Crafts
17 South Main Street
Lambertville, NJ 08530
(609) 397 9374
www.ragoarts.com
Galleries, antique shops,
Craftsman auctions.

Deby Zito
55 Bronte Street
San Francisco, CA 94110
(415) 648 6861

Gallery 532 Tribeca
142 Duane Street
New York, NY 10013
(212) 219 1327
Gallery featuring original Arts
& Crafts furniture, pottery,
lighting, metalwork.

Historic Lighting
114 East Lemon Avenue
Monrovia, CA 91016
(626) 303 4899
www.historiclighting.com
Gallery representing American
Craftsman, Arts & Crafts
Industries, Leick, Noble,
Production Furniture,
Royal Craftsman

J. Austin Antiques
1100 Cambridge St.
Cambridge, MA 02139
(617) 234 4444
Gallery devoted to Arts &
Crafts furniture, art pottery,
metalwork, and accessories.

James Ipekjian
Ipekjian Custom Wood Work
768 North Fair Oaks Avenue
Pasadena, CA 91103
(626) 792 5025

JMW Gallery
144 Lincoln Street
Boston, MA 02111
617 338 9097
Mission Oak furniture, and
American Arts & Crafts antiques
including art pottery, lighting,
metalwork, and textiles.

John Alexander Ltd
10–12 West Gravers Lane
Philadelpha, PA 19118
(215) 242 0741
www.johnalexanderltd.com
Furniture and decorative art
works from the English and
Scottish Arts & Crafts,
Gothic Revival, and
Aesthetic movements.

L. & J. G. Stickley, Inc.
One Stickley Drive
P.O. Box 480
Manlius, NY 13104-0480
(315) 682 5500
www.stickley.com
More than 500 different
reproduction furniture designs
based on Stickley originals.

The Mission Oak Shop
109 Main Street
Putnam, CT 06260
203 928 6662
Arts & Crafts furniture,
lighting, and accessories.

Old City Mission
162 North Third Street
Philadelphia, PA 19106
(215) 413 3040
American Arts & Crafts
furniture, pottery, metal,
lighting, and textiles.

Patrick Dickson
622 East Grinnell Drive
Burbank, CA 91501
(818) 846 4147

Restoration Hardware
15 Koch Road, Suite J.
Corte Madera, CA 94925-1240
(415) 924 1005 head office
(877) 747 4671 for stores
(800) 762 1005 for catalog
www.restorationhardware.com
Reproduction Arts & Crafts
furniture, lighting, fixtures.

Sam Mossaedi
P.O. Box 1221
La Canada, CA 91012
(818) 952 8454

Strictly Mission
3946 Lanark Road
Coopersburg, PA 18036
(610) 797 8640
www.strictlymission.com
Antiques and custom-made
reproductions.

Strictly Wood Furniture Co.
301 S. McDowell Street
Suite 811
Charlotte, NC 28204
(800) 278 2019
www.strictlywoodfurniture.
com
Mission-style furniture hand-
crafted from solid wood;
hardware, lighting, mirrors.

Thomas Stangeland
800 Mercer Street
Seattle, WA 98109
(206) 622 2004
www.artistcraftsman.net
Reproductions of Greenc and
Greene furniture.

Tim Gleason Gallery
77 Sullivan Street
New York, NY 10012
(212) 966 5777
Furniture, lighting and
accessories by Gustav Stickley
and his contemporaries.

Warren Hile Studio
1823 Enterprise Way
Monrovia, CA 91016
(626) 359 7210

Whit McLeod
P.O. Box 132
Arcata, CA 95518
(707) 825 7856

TEXTILES AND WALLPAPERS

Arts & Crafts Period Textiles
Dianne Ayres
5427 Telegraph Avenue #W2
Oakland, CA 94609
(510) 654 1645

**Bradbury & Bradbury
Art Wallpapers**
P.O. Box 155
Benicia, CA 94510
(707) 746 1900
www.bradbury.com
Hand-printed Arts & Crafts
wallpapers and borders by
mail order.

Charles Rupert Designs
2004 Oak Bay Avenue
Victoria, BC V8R 1E4
(250) 592 4916
www.charles-rupert.com
William Morris, Victorian, Arts &
Crafts and later periods, historic
wallpapers, fabrics, tiles, and home
accessories by mail order.

Inglenook Textiles
Ann Chaves
240 North Glendale Avenue
Pasadena, CA 91103
www.ITextiles@earthlink.net

J. R. Burrows & Co.
P.O. Box 522
Rockland
MA 02370
(800) 982 1812
English Arts & Crafts wallpapers,
including designs by Voysey;
William Morris carpets.

Liberty Valances and Curtains
768 North Fair Oaks
Pasadena, CA 91103
(626) 395 9997
Collection includes handcrafted
reproduction wooden curtain
valances from historic landmarks
such as The Gamble House.

Morrisstuff.com
1614 Gaylord St
Denver, CO 80206
(303) 377.0945;
www.morrisstuff.com
On-line store selling Morris & Co.
wallpapers, cotton prints, and
upholstery weaves.

Prairie Home Accents
3020 Legacy Drive, #100-369
Plano, TX 75023-8321
(972) 208 6338
www.prairiehomeaccents.com
Pillows and table linens in the Arts
& Crafts style.

Wallpaperguru
P.O. Box 491243
Los Angeles, CA 90049
(310) 281 6298
Installations and restorations of
antique, reproduction, and custom
wallpapers, murals, and fabrics.

LIGHTING

Arroyo Craftsman
4509 Little John Street
Baldwin Park, CA 91706
(626) 960 9411

Buffalo Studios
1925 Deere Avenue
Santa Ana
CA 92705
949 250 7333

Cherry Tree Designs
34154 East Frontage Road
Bozeman, MT 59715
(800) 634 3268
www.cherrytreedesign.com
Lighting fixtures made of wood
in the Arts & Crafts style.

Eastbay Sculpture & Lighting
4960 Allison Parkway, Unit C
Vacaville, CA 95688
(800) 447 2066

Historic Lighting
114 East Lemon Avenue
Monrovia, CA 91016
(626) 303 4899
Gallery representing Production,
Quizzed, Dale Tiffany, American
Deluxe.

James Matheson
10304 Hallandale Avenue
Tugging, CA 91042
(818) 352 9225

Jeff Grainger
2351 North Garfield Avenue
Altadena, CA 91001
(626) 798 2780

Karl Barry
265 Douglas Street
Brooklyn, NY 11217
(718) 596 1419

Mica Lamp Company
517 State Street
Glendale, CA 91203
(818) 241 7227

Phoenix Studios
10 Old Creamery Road
Harmony, CA 93435
(805) 927 4248

V. Michael Ashford
6543 Alpine Drive, SW
Olympia, WA 98512
(360) 352 0694
evergreenstudios.com
Hand-hammered copper
lighting and accessories.

William Morris
1716 Ellie Court
Benicia, CA 94510
(707) 745 3907

Yamagiwa USA Corporation
31340 Via Colinas, #106
Westlake Village, CA 91362
(888) 879 8611
Frank Lloyd Wright
reproductions.

ACCESSORIES

Anita Munman Design, Inc.
20th Century Fine Art
7727 North Ashland Avenue
Chicago, IL 60622
(773) 395 9992

Blue Mountain Pottery
21 Wild Wind Court
Saugerties, NY 12477
(845) 246 6952
www.bluemountainpots.com
Handmade pottery in Arts &
Crafts style.

Design Collections
Maclin Studio, Inc.
524 South 2nd Street
Milwaukee, WI 53204
(414) 276 4750
www.maclinstudio.com
Gifts and jewelry based on designs
by Frank Lloyd Wright and
Charles Rennie Mackintosh.

Donald Munz
314 May Avenue
Monrovia, CA 91016

DuQuella Tile & Clay Works
P.O. Box 90065
Portland, OR 97290-0065
(503) 256 8330
www.tiledecorative.com
Handcrafted tiles in Arts &
Crafts style to original designs.

Ephraim Faience Pottery
P.O. Box 792
Brookfield, WI 53008-0792
(888) 704 7687
www.ephraimpottery.com
Original and reproduction art
pottery, lamps, and tiles.

Hartwell Vintage Home
141 Elmgrove Avenue
Providence, RI 02906
(401) 273 7433
**www.hartwellvintagehome.
com**
Arts & Crafts era jewelry,
metalwork, lighting, textiles,
and pottery.

John Hamm
Hamm Glass
6310 Washington Avenue
Whittier, CA 90601
(562) 696 3364

Karen Michelle Antique Tiles
P.O. Box 489
Bridgewater, CT 06752
(860) 354 7197
Large stock of antique art tiles
and fireplace surrounds.

Kathleen West
159 Maple Street
East Aurora, NY 14052
(716) 652 9125

Lundberg Glass
131 Old Coast Road
Davenport, CA 95017
(831) 423 2532

Motawi Tileworks
33 North Staebler #2
Ann Arbor, MI 48103
(734) 213 0017

Nature's Loom
32 East 31st Street
New York, New York 10016
(212) 686 2002
www.naturesloom.com
Rugs in Arts & Crafts style.

Nichibei Potters
1991 Burnside Road
Sebastopol, CA 95472
707 823 0950
www.nichibeipotters.com
Handmade pottery that blends
Arts & Crafts and traditional
Japanese styles.

Once Upon A Tile
2720 Higbee
Memphis, TN 38111
(901) 327 7179
Reproductions of Arts &
Crafts tile designs.

Ray West
1681 Coy Flat Drive
Camp Nelson
Springville, CA 93265
(559) 542 2203

Susan Herbert Imports
1231 NW Hoyt Street #B-5
Portland, OR 97209
(503) 248 1111

Ted Harper
15 Great Glen Road
Greenville, SC 29615
(864) 268 2982

Tile Restoration Center, Inc.
3511 Interlake North
Seattle, WA 98103
(206) 633 4866
www.tilerestorationcenter.com
Specializing in recreating the
methods, designs, and colors of
the tiles of Ernest Batchelder.

PICTURE CREDITS

All photographs by Andrew Wood unless otherwise stated.
a = above, **b** = below, **c** = center, **l** = left, **r** = right.

Endpapers Tim Ractliff, Little Thakeham in West Sussex, designed by Edwin Lutyens 1902–3; **1** photographer Polly Wreford/Sheila Scholes & Gunter Schmidt's house in Cambridgeshire; **2** The King House in Mammoth Lakes, California; **3** Curtice Booth's house in Pasadena, California; **4–5** Tim Ractliff, Little Thakeham in West Sussex, designed by Edwin Lutyens 1902–3; **6–7** photographer Polly Wreford/Sheila Scholes & Gunter Schmidt's house in Cambridgeshire; **8–9** The King House in Mammoth Lakes, California; **10–11** The Pasadena, California, home of Susan D'Avignon; **12–13** Sally & Ian's home in England; **14** The Pasadena, California, home of Susan D'Avignon; **15** Tim Ractliff, Little Thakeham in West Sussex, designed by Edwin Lutyens 1902–3; **16** "Spartina" on Fisher's Island, New York, designed by Michael Farewell FAIA of Ford Farewell Mills & Gatsch Architects; **17 l** Paul & Carolyn Morgan's house in Wales; **17 r** Sally & Ian's home in England; **18 l** An Apartment in New York designed by Stephen Shadley; **18 c & r** Philip & Barbara Silver's house in Idaho designed by Mark Pynn AIA of McMillen Pynn Architecture LLP; **19** Randell L. Makinson House, Pasadena, California. Design: Buff & Hensman FAIA & Randall L. Makinson, Hon. AIA, Associated Architects; **20–21** "Spartina" on Fisher's Island, New York, designed by Michael Farewell FAIA of Ford Farewell Mills & Gatsch Architects; **22–23** The Caroline Deforest House in Pasadena, California, home of Michael Murray and Kelly Jones; **24–27** Paul & Carolyn Morgan's house in Wales; **28–29** "Spartina" on Fisher's Island, New York, designed by Michael Farewell, FAIA of Ford Farewell Mills & Gatsch Architects; **30–31** Curtice Booth's house in Pasadena, California; **32–33** Duncan-Irwin House in Pasadena, California, home of André & Ann Chaves; **34** Pete & Connie di Girolamo house in San Diego, California; **35** The Los Angeles home of Pat & Jane Qualey; **36** Philip & Barbara Silver's house in Idaho designed by Mark Pynn AIA of McMillen Pynn Architecture LLP; **37** The Glendale, California, home of John & Heather Banfield; **38** An Apartment in New York designed by Stephen Shadley; **39** Anthony & Julia Collett's house in London designed by Anthony Collett of Collett Zarzycki Ltd; **40–41** photographer Polly Wreford/Sheila Scholes & Gunter Schmidt's house in Cambridgeshire; **42** The Pasadena, California, home of Susan D'Avignon; **43 bl & br** Tim Ractliff, Little Thakeham in West Sussex, designed by Edwin Lutyens 1902–3; **43 ar** The King House in Mammoth Lakes, California; **44** Duncan-Irwin House in Pasadena, California, home of André & Ann Chaves; **45** Lynn & Linda's home in Cambria, California; **46 al & ar** Pete & Connie di Girolamo house in San Diego, California; **46 b** The Shell House, California, home of Chuck and Evelyn Plemons; **47** The Caroline Deforest House in Pasadena, California, home of Michael Murray and Kelly Jones; **48 l** An Apartment in New York designed by Stephen Shadley; **48–49** Anthony & Julia Collett's house in London designed by Anthony Collett of Collett Zarzycki Ltd; **50** Randell L. Makinson house, Pasadena, California. Design: Buff & Hensman FAIA & Randall L. Makinson, Hon. AIA, Associated Architects; **51 l & r** Philip & Barbara Silver's house in Idaho designed by Mark Pynn AIA of McMillen Pynn Architecture LLP; **52–53** The Caroline Deforest House in Pasadena, California, home of Michael Murray and Kelly Jones; **54 la, lc & lb** Pete & Connie di Girolamo house in San Diego, California; **54–55 main** Duncan-Irwin House in Pasadena, California, home of André & Ann Chaves; **55 r** The Shell House, California, home of Chuck and Evelyn Plemons; **56 al & bl** Philip & Barbara Silver's house in Idaho designed by Mark Pynn AIA of McMillen Pynn Architecture LLP; **56–57 main & 57** Anthony & Julia Collett's house in London designed by Anthony Collett of Collett Zarzycki Ltd; **58–59** The home of Gwen Aldridge and Bruce McLucas; **60–61** Curtice Booth's house in Pasadena, California; **62–63** Pete & Connie di Girolamo house in San Diego, California; **64–65** The Caroline Deforest House in Pasadena, California, home of Michael Murray and Kelly Jones; **65** "Spartina" on Fisher's Island, New York, designed by Michael Farewell FAIA of Ford Farewell Mills & Gatsch Architects; **66** The King House in Mammoth Lakes, California; **68–69** The Glendale, California, home of John & Heather Banfield; **70–71** Paul & Carolyn Morgan's house in Wales; **72 & 73 l** The Caroline Deforest House in Pasadena, California, home of Michael Murray and Kelly Jones; **73 r** The Shell House, California, home of Chuck and Evelyn Plemons; **74 l** Lynn & Linda's home in Cambria, California; **74–75 c** The Pasadena, California, home of Susan D'Avignon; **75 al & ar** The King House in Mammoth Lakes, California; **75 b** Pete & Connie di Girolamo house in San Diego, California; **76–77** Anthony & Julia Collett's house in London designed by Anthony Collett of Collett Zarzycki Ltd; **77 r** photographer Chris Everard/Mark Kirkley & Harumi Kaijima's house in Sussex; **77 br** photographer Polly Wreford/Sheila Scholes & Gunter Schmidt's house in Cambridgeshire; **78** Curtice Booth's house in Pasadena, California; **79–80** The King House in Mammoth Lakes, California; **81** The Pasadena, California, home of Susan D'Avignon; **82–83** Tim Ractliff, Little Thakeham in West Sussex, designed by Edwin Lutyens 1902–3; **84 al & bl** The Shell House, California, home of Chuck and Evelyn Plemons; **84 ac & br** The Los Angeles home of Pat & Jane Qualey; **84 ar** Pete & Connie di Girolamo house in San Diego, California; **85** Philip & Barbara Silver's house in Idaho designed by Mark Pynn AIA of McMillen Pynn Architecture LLP; **86** The King House in Mammoth Lakes,

California; **87** Lynn & Linda's home in Cambria, California; **88 al & ar** The Shell House, California, home of Chuck and Evelyn Plemons, **88 br & 89 r** Paul & Carolyn Morgan's house in Wales; **89 l** "Spartina" on Fisher's Island, New York, designed by Michael Farewell FAIA of Ford Farewell Mills & Gatsch Architects; **90 al** photographer Polly Wreford/Sheila Scholes & Gunter Schmidt's house in Cambridgeshire; **91** Paul & Carolyn Morgan's house in Wales; **92–93 main** Duncan-Irwin House in Pasadena, California, home of André & Ann Chaves; **93 al** Lynn & Linda's home in Cambria, California; **93 ar** "Spartina" on Fisher's Island, New York, designed by Michael Farewell FAIA of Ford Farewell Mills & Gatsch Architects; **93 br** photographer Chris Everard/Mark Kirkley & Harumi Kaijima's house in Sussex; **94 l & 95** Tim Ractliff, Little Thakeham, West Sussex, designed by Edwin Lutyens 1902–3; **94 c & r** photographer Chris Everard/Mark Kirkley & Harumi Kaijima's house in Sussex; **96–97** Duncan-Irwin House in Pasadena, California, home of André & Ann Chaves; **98 al & ar** photographer Chris Everard/Mark Kirkley & Harumi Kaijima's house in Sussex; **98c** photographer Polly Wreford/Sheila Scholes & Gunter Schmidt's house in Cambridgeshire; **98 b** Philip & Barbara Silver's house in Idaho designed by Mark Pynn AIA of McMillen Pynn Architecture LLP; **99** Anthony & Julia Collett's house in London designed by Anthony Collett of Collett Zarzycki Ltd; **100–101** photographer Polly Wreford/Sheila Scholes & Gunter Schmidt's house in Cambridgeshire; **102 l** The Glendale, California, home of John & Heather Banfield; **102–103 c** photographer Chris Everard/Mark Kirkley & Harumi Kaijima's house in Sussex; **103 al 95** Tim Ractliff, Little Thakeham, West Sussex, designed by Edwin Lutyens 1902–3; **103 bl & ar** photographer Polly Wreford/Sheila Scholes & Gunter Schmidt's house in Cambridgeshire; **103 br** Lynn & Linda's home in Cambria, California; **104 al** The Pasadena, California, home of Susan D'Avignon; **104 bl** photographer Chris Everard/Mark Kirkley & Harumi Kaijima's house in Sussex; **104–105 c** Pete & Connie di Girolamo house in San Diego, California; **105 al & b** photographer Chris Everard/Mark Kirkley & Harumi Kaijima's house in Sussex; **105 ar** Philip & Barbara Silver's house in Idaho designed by Mark Pynn AIA of McMillen Pynn Architecture LLP; **106 & 107 l** Tim Ractliff, Little Thakeham, West Sussex, designed by Edwin Lutyens 1902–3; **107 ac & 108 b** Philip & Barbara Silver's house in Idaho designed by Mark Pynn AIA of McMillen Pynn Architecture LLP; **107 ar & br** photographer Chris Everard/Mark Kirkley & Harumi Kaijima's house in Sussex; **107 bc** Sally & Ian's home in England; **108 t & 109** "Spartina" on Fisher's Island, New York, designed by Michael Farewell FAIA of Ford Farewell Mills & Gatsch Architects; **110 a & 111 r** The Pasadena, California, home of Susan D'Avignon; **110 bl & br** An Apartment in New York designed by Stephen Shadley; **112** Tim Ractliff, Little Thakeham, West Sussex, designed by Edwin Lutyens 1902–3; **113** Anthony & Julia Collett's house in London designed by Anthony Collett of Collett Zarzycki Ltd;

114 b & 115 bl & br photographer Chris Everard/Mark Kirkley & Harumi Kaijima's house in Sussex; **114–115 c & ar** Curtice Booth's house in Pasadena, California; **116 l** Anthony & Julia Collett's house in London designed by Anthony Collett of Collett Zarzycki Ltd; **116 r** Curtice Booth's house in Pasadena, California; **117** The Glendale, California, home of John & Heather Banfield; **118** photographer Polly Wreford/Sheila Scholes & Gunter Schmidt's house in Cambridgeshire; **119** The Glendale, California, home of John & Heather Banfield; **120** "Spartina" on Fisher's Island, New York, designed by Michael Farewell FAIA of Ford Farewell Mills & Gatsch Architects; **121 al & bc** photographer Polly Wreford/Sheila Scholes & Gunter Schmidt's house in Cambridgeshire; **121 ac & bl** The Glendale, California, home of John & Heather Banfield; **121 ar** Tim Ractliff, Little Thakeham, West Sussex, designed by Edwin Lutyens 1902–3; **121 cr** photographer Chris Everard/Mark Kirkley & Harumi Kaijima's house in Sussex; **122 al** Pete & Connie di Girolamo house in San Diego, California; **122 r** Paul & Carolyn Morgan's house in Wales; **123 ar & bc** The Pasadena, California, home of Susan D'Avignon; **123 bl** The home of Gwen Aldridge and Bruce McLucas; **123 br** Lynn & Linda's home in Cambria, California; **124 l & ar** Curtice Booth's house in Pasadena, California; **124 bl & br** The Caroline Deforest House in Pasadena, California, home of Michael Murray and Kelly Jones, **126 & 127 ar & cr** The King House in Mammoth Lakes, California; **127 l** Paul & Carolyn Morgan's house in Wales; **127 br** The Pasadena, California, home of Susan D'Avignon; **128 al** Randell L. Makinson house, Pasadena, California. Design: Buff & Hensman FAIA & Randall L. Makinson, Hon. AIA, Associated Architects; **128 ar** Duncan-Irwin House in Pasadena, California, home of André & Ann Chaves; **128 bl** Paul & Carolyn Morgan's house in Wales; **128 br & 129 br** "Spartina" on Fisher's Island, New York, designed by Michael Farewell FAIA of Ford Farewell Mills & Gatsch Architects; **129 l** The Shell House, California, home of Chuck and Evelyn Plemons; **129 ar** The Los Angeles home of Pat & Jane Qualey; **130** The Pasadena, California, home of Susan D'Avignon; **131 al, bl & br** The Glendale, California, home of John & Heather Banfield; **131 ar** The home of Gwen Aldridge and Bruce McLucas; **132 & 133 bl** The Pasadena, California, home of Susan D'Avignon; **133 ar** The Caroline Deforest House in Pasadena, California, home of Michael Murray and Kelly Jones; **133 br** Sally & Ian's home in England; **134 & 135 l** "Spartina" on Fisher's Island, New York, designed by Michael Farewell FAIA of Ford Farewell Mills & Gatsch Architects; **135 r** Lynn & Linda's home in Cambria, California; **136 al** The Glendale, California, home of John & Heather Banfield; **136 b** "Spartina" on Fisher's Island, New York, designed by Michael Farewell FAIA of Ford Farewell Mills & Gatsch Architects; **137 l** Duncan-Irwin House in Pasadena, California, home of André & Ann Chaves; **137 ar** Curtice Booth's house in Pasadena, California; **137 br** Pete & Connie di Girolamo house in San Diego, California.

ARCHITECTS & DESIGNERS WHOSE WORK IS FEATURED IN THIS BOOK

Anthony Collett
Collett Zarzycki Ltd
Fernhead Studios
2b Fernhead Road
London W9 3ET
United Kingdom
t. + 44 20 8969 6967
f. + 44 20 8960 6480
e. mail@czltd.co.uk

Mark Pynn AIA
McMillen Pynn
    Architecture LLP
P.O. Box 1068
Sun Valley
Idaho 83353
t. (208) 622 4656
f. (208) 726 7108
e. mpynn@sunvalley.net

Sheila Scholes
Designer
t. + 44 1480 498 241

Stephen Shadley Designs
144 West 27th Street
New York, NY 10001
t. (212) 243 6913
f. (212) 627 3303

Michael Farewell
Ford Farewell Mills &
    Gatsch Architects
101 Carnegie Center
Suite 301
Princeton
NJ 08540-6235

Randell L. Makinson
RLM Associates
Restoration Consultants
f. (626) 449 2059
e. makinson@earthlink.net

SOURCES

Charlieroe
91 Corhampton Road
Bournemouth
Dorset BH6 5NX
United Kingdom
t/f. + 44 1202 469576
e. info@charlieroe.com
www.charlieroe.com

Hill House Antiques
P.O. Box 17320
London SW3 2WR
United Kingdom
t. + 44 20 7581 3918
e. sbhhouse@aol.com

Mark Kirkley
designer & manufacturer
of interior metalwork
t/f. + 44 1424 812613

**The Arts & Crafts
Furniture Company**
49 Sheen Lane
London SW14 8AB
United Kingdom
t. + 44 20 8876 6544
e. acfc@49sheen.fsnet.co.uk

LAMPS AND METALWORK
(as featured in
Paul Morgan's house)

Jonathan Cooke
Nantcol Works
Llanbedr
Gwynedd LL45 2NP
United Kingdom
t. + 44 1341 241587

WELSH OAK FURNITURE
(Paul Morgan's house)

Bernard Harman
also at Nantcol Works
Llanbedr
Gwynedd LL45 2NP
United Kingdom
t. + 44 1341 241587

STAINED GLASS
(Paul Morgan's house)

**Abbott Jones Design
Partnership**
The Outbuildings
Fron Dirion
Mynydd Mechell
Amlwch
Anglesey LL68 OTE
United Kingdom
t. + 44 1407 710928

CLASSICAL GLASS
(Paul Morgan's house)

Woodstock
Llanrwst Road
Glan Conwy
Gwynedd LL28 5SR
United Kingdom
t. + 44 1492 580454

**EMBROIDERY AND
HANGINGS**
(Paul Morgan's house)

Jean Salt
t. + 44 1766 770801

INDEX

Page numbers in italics refer to captions/illustrations only.